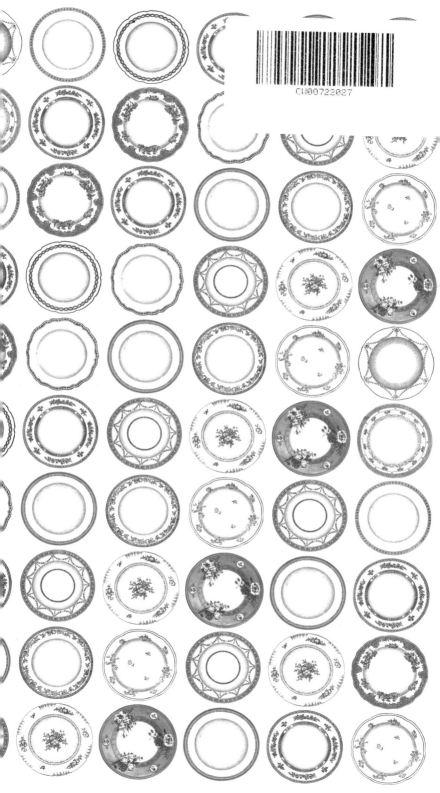

irene's
peranakan
recipes

memories & recipes

"Girls have to do girls' things."

With her cherished recipe for womanhood, Mother strived to be a super woman and came pretty close.

My mother, **irene**

SHE THREW HERSELF INTO COOKING, sewing, flower arrangement and gardening. Her two fiercest passions – which I never inherited – were cooking and flower arrangement. She sewed almost anything and everything she could get her hands on: the curtains in the house, fancy clothes for my sister and me, our school uniforms. She arranged flowers to transform the house, landscaped our garden, and entertained friends with her famed cooking – on top of a full-time job. Thinking about Mother exhausts me. And yes, she was the disciplinarian in the family.

She was also the president of the North Division of the Singapore Girl Guides Association even though she had never been a Guide. She was the vice-president of the Women's Society of Christian Services (WSCS) in the Methodist Church in Singapore, in which she travelled all over the world attending conferences. She was also one of the founding members of the Glowing Years Ministry (GYM) of the Methodist Church, and was president of the Ang Mo Kio Methodist Church WSCS and Senior Fellowship for many years. All this obviously kept her busy, but she held on to her two passions. And boy, how she pursued them to the end.

She took flower arrangement classes soon after marrying my dad and before long she was beautifying the church with fresh blooms. Friends admired her work so much, they started asking her to do weddings and other functions. She did this till retirement, when she started a flower business with my dad.

Her cooking and baking skills were also well known. She loved to cook for others, and enjoyed having them gush over her food. She often entertained at home. When invited over to her friend's place, she would take a home-cooked dish. Mee siam was her signature dish, and all my friends used to jump at the chance of being invited home for dinner, especially if mee siam was on the menu. Many of her fans would eat mee siam only when cooked by her. Her beef rendang was another specialty. In her younger days, it was not uncommon for the family to host parties for 40 to 50 people at a time, and she would single-handedly cook for everyone. That was a far cry from when she couldn't even cook rice.

Mother came from a quintessentially Teochew family. The household was marshalled by my late grandmother, who was the 'highest authority in the land' and would not tolerate any of her six children in the kitchen. They had servants to do all the housework and cooking under her strict supervision. When my mother got married at the age of 24, she could cook nothing. My father had to teach her the few simple dishes that he knew, and they got by eating simply. My mother knew that she had to do something about it.

My Family

My father came from a traditional Peranakan family. They spoke Nonya-Malay at home, and the Peranakan culture was ingrained in their upbringing. His mother was a great cook, but unfortunately both parents passed away before he was out of his teens. Since my dad knew what good Nonya food was, it was only natural that he wanted my mum to whip up the traditional Nonya dishes that he so loved. Mother enrolled in cooking classes and the rest is history and gravy.

Through trial and error, swapping recipes with friends, bombarding cooking classes, gleaning cooking tips from neighbours and friends... and also my father's discerning taste buds, my mother's culinary genie emerged.

My dad was always very supportive. He would accompany her to the market, helping her buy the freshest ingredients. In the kitchen, you would find him cutting, dicing, pounding and washing. Maybe that was his way of working up a big appetite.

Mother loved nothing more than delving hungrily into cookbooks. She had piles of them, always on her bedside table, which she would read in bed before sleeping. She never found the time for fiction or non-fiction. She relished comparing recipes, taking notes, and bringing them to life in her magical kingdom, or rather, kitchen. She was on a perpetual quest for the perfect recipe, or simply a new one. Even on holiday trips abroad, it was normal for my mother to talk to the restaurant chef if she enjoyed the food. On one Tasmanian trip, she woke up at 4am to help the bakers at the local bakery prepare bread for the start of the day.

When my sister and I were planning to go to the UK for further studies, my mother decided to compile all the recipes of the dishes we had grown to love. She wanted us to take the recipes with us, and hopefully be able to cook some of our family favourites while we were there. It took her many moons to write and compile them.

Having done so, she decided to put them to good use. As she was already 55, and planning for retirement at that time, she thought of starting her own cooking class. After years of cooking for others, and knowing how much people loved her food, she was confident it would fly. In fact, the fear of failure was rarely on her menu.

She planned the recipes meticulously. With a balanced course, she placed her first advertisement in the Straits Times Classifieds. Ten ladies attended her first class. With that fillip, she began to teach on a regular basis. People from all walks of life passed through her kitchen. Impeccable tai-tais, clueless newly-wed wives, Filipino maids, and tough guys with a soft spot for cooking. She even taught a few students who went on to open stalls selling Nonya food based on her recipes. I attended a few of her classes, and her students really had quite a good time, not only learning how to cook, but socialising and making new friends.

As word of her cooking classes spread, organisations started approaching her to conduct classes for them. She taught at classes organised by the Social Development Unit, the Welfare Club of Tan Tock Seng Hospital and church groups. With all these classes, she was able to fine-tune her recipes even further. She enjoyed sharing her cooking skills with others, and never withheld any 'secrets'; her students always came back for more. Which resonated nicely with those of us at home.

You see, Mother would always cooked an extra portion for us the day she had classes. So we always wanted to know which dish she was going to teach for the day. Somehow, the dishes tasted better. Perhaps it was because she was 'guided' by her own recipes!

Writing a cookbook had always stimulated and eluded Mother. With her busy schedule, her church work, the flower business, and being a full-time grandmother to my sister's three beautiful children, the aspiration just slipped by. We feel that perhaps it would be good to share with you some recipes of the family's favourite dishes. Now that we have finally managed to get this little cookbook published, I hope that this will bring joy to those who try cooking these recipes, as much as she enjoyed cooking them herself.

And oh, feel free to improvise and improve on the recipes. Because there's no better appetizer than a sprinkling of your own delicious imagination.

Elaine Yeo

Contents

Soup

Hee Peow Soup 12

Sotong Soup 13

Bakwan Kepeting 14

Poultry

Ayam Assam Tumis 18

Petis Hati 19

Curry Ayam 20

Ayam Siyow 21

Satay Ayam Rebus 22

Gulai Ayam Kunyit 23

Ayam Buah Keluak 24

Itek Tim 26

Itek Chin 27

Meat

Satay Ayam or Satay Babi 32

Satay Lembu or Satay Kambing 34

Satay Babi Rebus 35

Penang Nonya Ngoh Hiang 36

Penang Nonya Deep Fried Cha Shao 37

Babi Panggang 38

Babi Assam 39

Seafood

Assam Sotong Goreng 44

Sambal Sotong Goreng 45

Sambal Sotong Sumbat 46

Assam Udang Goreng 47

Gulai Lemak Nanas 48

Sambal Udang 49

Udang Garam Assam 50

Udang Goreng Chilli 51

Udang Goreng 52

Udang Pedas Nanas 53

Sambal Udang Kering 54

Ikan Curry 55

Gulai Ikan Assam 56

Ikan Gulai Penang 57

Kuah Ladah 58

Otak Otak 59

Sambal Lengkong 60

irene's peranakan recipes

Published by Epigram – 75 Sophia Road Singapore 228156. Tel 65-6292 4456. Fax 65-6292 4414. www.epigram.com.sg
Copyright©2006 Epigram. All rights reserved. No part of this publication may be reproduced without prior consent from the publisher.
Second printing, 2007.
Printed in Singapore.
National Library Board Singapore Cataloguing in Publication Data
Irene, 1938-2004.
    Irene's Peranakan Recipes. – Singapore : Epigram, c2006.
    p. cm.
    ISBN-13 : 978-981-05-7015-6
    ISBN-10: 981-05-7015-5

    1. Cookery, Peranakan. I. Title.
TX724.5.S55
641.595957 -- dc22   SLS2006047186

EPIGRAM BOOKS

Vegetables

Chap Chye 64
Fried Kiam Chye ... 65
Gado Gado 66
Sambal Terong
Bendi 68
Sambal Tau Kwa ... 69
Tau Kwa Goreng ... 70
Sambal Timun 71
Kueh Pie Tee 72
Achar with
Rempah 74

Padang

Ikan Masak
Lemak Kuning 80
Ikan Goreng
Berlada 81
Ikan Bakar 82
Ikan Gulai 83
Ikan Masak
Lemak Merah 84
Ikan Frikkadels 85
Fried Ikan Bilis 86
Chicken Korma 87
Ayam Pangang 88
Ayam Masak
Merah 89
Ayam Goreng
Padang 90
Ayam Rendang 92
Rendang Padang ... 93
Curry Kambing 94
Daging
Panggang 95
Udang Kelio 96
Sotong Sambal 97
Sayur Loday 98
Terong Goreng 99
Sambal Telur 100
Sambal Kachang
Panjang 101
Kachang Panjang
Goreng 102
Achar Nanas 103
Achar Bening 104

Rice & Noodles

Nasi Lemak 108
Nasi Kunyit 109
Mee Siam 110
Mee Rebus 112
Laksa 114

Kueh

Kueh Ubi
Kayu Kelapa 120
Kueh Gula Melaka
Ubi Kayu 121
Kueh Ubi
Kayu Rebus 122
Kueh Talam
Ubi Kayu 123
Kueh Keria 124
Kueh Bingkah 125
Lepat Ubi Kayu ... 126
Lepat Pisang 127
Goreng Pisang 128
Kueh Pisang (Kueh
Naga Sari) 129
Kueh Kodok 130
Seri Kaya 131
Sago Gula
Melaka 132
Abok-Abok
Sago 133
Pulut Terigu 134
Pulut Inti 135
Pengat 136
Kueh Wajek 137
Kueh Sarlat 138
Kueh Dadar 140
Kueh Lapis 142
Kueh Lapis
Beras 143
Kueh Kosui 144
Iced Delima 145
Bubor Pulut
Hitam 146
Bubor Kachang
Hijau 147
Bubor Cha-Cha with
Pisang Raja 148
Pengat Pisang
Durian 149
Ang Koo Kueh 150
Onde-Onde 152

Soup

HEE PEOW SOUP
CABBAGE, MEAT AND PRAWNBALL SOUP

(A):

80	gm fried fish bladder (hee peow) soaked in warm water, washed and cut into pieces
500	gm cabbage (cut into square pieces)
3	ℓ stock (boiled from 500gm pork bones)
¼	tsp salt

Meatball mixture (B):

150	gm minced pork
150	gm fish paste
1	clove garlic (chopped and fried)
1	egg white
¼	tsp pepper

Prawnball mixture (C):

100	gm prawns (shelled and minced)
100	gm fish paste
1	clove garlic (chopped and fried)
1	egg white
¼	tsp pepper

Garnish:
coriander leaves

Put ingredients (B) into a bowl. Mix thoroughly. Take a lump of the mixture and form into a ball, hitting it onto the palm of the hand till firm (better if your palm is slightly oiled). Repeat for the rest of the mixture. Do the same for ingredients (C).

Pour the stock into a large pot. Add the cabbage and bring to a boil. Add the meatballs (B), the prawnballs (C) and the fried fish bladder. Add salt to taste. Lower the heat and simmer till the cabbage softens. (Meatballs are cooked when they float to the surface.)

Serve hot and garnish with coriander leaves.

SOTONG SOUP
SOUP WITH STUFFED SQUID

(A):

300	gm squid
2	cloves garlic (chopped)
15	gm fine glass noodles (tung hoon)
1	stalk spring onion (cut into pieces)
1	sprig parsley (cut into pieces)
450	mℓ water
1	tsp light soy sauce
	cooking oil

Stuffing (B):

150	gm minced pork
½	tsp light soy sauce
¼	tsp pepper
¼	tsp corn flour

Garnish:
spring onions
parsley

To prepare the squid: Remove the head and eyes of the squid, pull out the bone and the ink sac. Discard. Peel off the outer reddish layer of the skin. Rinse well, washing away all traces of ink. Wash in salt water.

Drain and set aside.

To cook: Heat a soup pot till hot, then add the oil. When it is hot, add the chopped garlic and stir fry till golden brown. Remove the fried garlic from the oil and add it to the stuffing (B). Leave the garlic oil for the soup preparation.

Mix the meat stuffing with the soya sauce, pepper and corn flour (B). Stuff each squid with this meat mixture. With the remaining meat mixture, form meatballs, firmly patting each one.

Pour the water into the soup pot (into the remaining garlic oil) and bring to a boil. Add the stuffed squid and meatballs. Next, add the glass noodles and the light soy sauce. Lower the heat and simmer for 5 minutes.

Serve garnished with spring onions and parsley.

BAKWAN KEPETING
MEATBALL AND BAMBOO SHOOT SOUP

Meatball mixture (A):

- 250 gm minced pork
- 250 gm minced fish paste
- 200 gm crab meat
- 50 gm bamboo shoots (finely shredded and chopped)
- 1 egg
- 1 tsp light soy sauce
- 2 cloves garlic (chopped)
- 2 tbsps cooking oil

Soup (B):

- 2 ℓ stock (boiled from 500gm pork bones)
- 1 tsp salt
- 200 gm bamboo shoots (shredded)
- garlic oil

Garnish:

coriander leaves

Heat a saucepan till hot, then add the oil. When it is hot, add the chopped garlic and stir fry till golden brown. Remove the fried garlic from the oil and add it to the meatball mixture (A). Leave the garlic oil for the soup preparation.

Place all the ingredients (A) into a large mixing bowl. Mix well.

Take a lump of the meatball mixture and form into a ball, hitting it onto the palm of the hand till firm (better if your hand is slightly oiled). Repeat for the rest of the mixture. Set aside.

Using the garlic oil, stir fry the bamboo shoots (B) for 2 minutes. Remove and set aside. Pour the stock into a large soup pot. Bring to a boil. Add the meatballs, then the fried bamboo shoots. Add the salt. Turn down the heat and simmer for 10 minutes.

Garnish the soup with coriander leaves and serve with sambal belachan.

Shopping list:

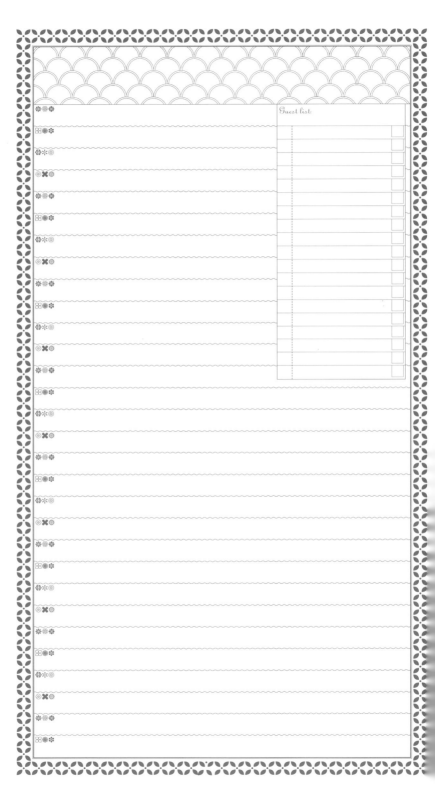

Guest list:

Poultry

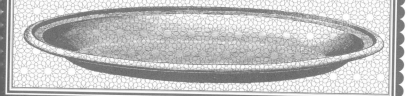

AYAM ASSAM TUMIS
CHICKEN PREPARED IN TAMARIND GRAVY

   1   chicken (1½kg) cut into serving pieces
   1   tbsp tamarind (mixed with 450mℓ water,
       strain liquid for use)
  ½   tbsp sugar
   1   tsp salt
   4   tbsps cooking oil

Grind together:
10-15   dried chillies (soaked, washed and seeded)
   3   cm length galangal
   3   cm length tumeric
   2   stalks lemon grass (discard outer green layer,
       use white portion only)
   1   stalk bunga kantan (phaeomaria or pink ginger bud)
 10   shallots
   4   cloves garlic
   1   tsp shrimp paste (belachan)

Heat a saucepan till hot, then add the oil. When the oil is hot, add the ground ingredients.

Stir fry till fragrant. Add the chicken pieces and stir fry for a few minutes. Next, add the tamarind water and bring to a boil. Season with sugar and salt.

Lower the heat and simmer till chicken is tender.

PETIS HATI
SPICY CHICKEN LIVER

300	gm chicken liver
2	tbsps coriander powder
1	tsp cumin powder
1	tsp brown sugar
½	tsp tamarind (mixed with 2 tsps water, strain liquid for use)
10	green chillies (sliced)
¼	tsp salt
	cooking oil
1	tbsp water

Grind together:

3	stalks lemon grass (discard outer green layer, use white portion only)
3	cloves garlic
1	big onion
8	dried red chillies
3	cm length ginger
3	cm length galangal
½	tsp shrimp paste (belachan)

To prepare the chicken liver: Wash the liver in salt water and parboil with water. Drain dry and cut into cubes.

To cook: Heat the saucepan till hot, then add the oil. When the oil is hot, add the ground ingredients, as well as the coriander and cumin powder. Stir fry till fragrant.

Add the chicken liver and water. Stir fry for a while. When the liver is tender, add the tamarind water and brown sugar, sliced green chillies and salt. Simmer till the gravy thickens.

CURRY AYAM
CHICKEN CURRY

1	chicken (1½kg) cut into serving pieces
500	gm potatoes (skinned, quartered and soaked in salt water)
4	shallots (sliced)
4	cloves garlic (sliced)
1	cm length ginger (cut into strips)
3	tbsps curry powder (mixed with 4 tbsps water to form a paste)
900	ml coconut milk (add 750ml water to 1 grated coconut, squeeze mixture for coconut milk)
½	tsp salt
6	tbsps cooking oil

Heat a saucepan till hot, add the oil. Add the potatoes and fry till lightly browned. Set aside.

With the leftover oil, stir fry the ginger, garlic and shallots till golden brown. Add the curry powder paste and stir fry till fragrant. Add the chicken pieces. Continue to stir fry for another 5 minutes, before pouring in half the coconut milk.

Simmer for a while before pouring in the other half. Stir well and bring to a boil. Add the potatoes. Lower the heat and simmer till the chicken and potatoes are cooked. Season with salt.

AYAM SIYOW
SPICY CHICKEN IN THICK TAMARIND SAUCE

(A):
- 1 chicken (1½kg) cut into serving pieces
- 2 tbsps cooking oil

Marinade (B):
- 2 tbsps tamarind (mixed with 450mℓ water, strain liquid for use)
- 10 shallots (ground)
- 1 tbsp toasted coriander powder
- 1½ tbsps sugar
- 1 tbsp dark soy sauce
- ½ tbsp vinegar
- 1 tsp salt
- 1 tsp pepper

Garnish:
cucumber (sliced)

Marinate the chicken pieces with the marinade ingredients (B). Leave aside for several hours.

Place the chicken pieces and the marinade in a stewing pot and bring to a boil, uncovered.

Simmer till the chicken is tender. Remove the chicken pieces from the saucepan and set aside. Allow the gravy to continue to simmer till it thickens.

Heat the oil in another saucepan and when it is hot, add the chicken pieces. Over low heat, fry the chicken pieces till golden brown. Add the thickened gravy to the chicken pieces.

Serve garnished with cucumber slices.

SATAY AYAM REBUS
BOILED SPICED CHICKEN

(A):
- 1   chicken (1½kg) cut into serving pieces
- 550   ml coconut milk (add 450ml water to ½ grated coconut, squeeze mixture for coconut milk)

Marinade (B):
- 1   tsp salt
- 1   tsp sugar
- ½   tsp pepper powder
- 1   tsp coriander powder

Grind together (C):
- 4   stalks lemon grass (discard outer green layer, use white portion only)
- 8   fresh red chillies (seeded)
- 8   dried red chillies (soaked, washed and seeded)
- 4   candlenuts
- 16   shallots
- 1   tsp shrimp paste (belachan)

Marinate the chicken pieces with ingredients (B). Set aside for 1 hour.

Place all the ingredients (A), (B) and (C) into a saucepan. Bring to a boil. Lower the heat and simmer till the chicken is cooked and the sauce thickens.

GULAI AYAM KUNYIT
SPICY CHICKEN ON YELLOW RICE

  1   chicken (1½kg) cut into serving pieces
800   mℓ coconut milk (add 675mℓ water to 1 grated coconut,
      squeeze mixture for coconut milk)
  3   whole cloves
  2   sticks cinnamon (6cm length)
  2   star anise
  1   stalk lemon grass (bruised, discard outer green layer,
      use white portion only)
  ½   tsp salt

Grind together:
 12   dried chillies (soaked, washed and seeded)
  6   cm length tumeric
  3   cm length ginger
 12   shallots
  4   cloves garlic
  1   stalk lemon grass (bruised)

Add:
  1   tbsp coriander powder
  ½   tsp cumin powder

Heat the saucepan till hot, then add the oil. When the oil is hot, add the ground ingredients as well as the coriander powder and cumin powder. Stir fry the ground ingredients till fragrant. Add a few tablespoons of coconut milk to keep the mixture moist. Stir fry for another minute.

Add the chicken pieces. Stir fry till they are well coated with the ground ingredients. Add 2-3 tablespoons of coconut milk and stir fry for another 3 minutes. Pour in the remaining coconut milk till the chicken is immersed. Add the salt, star anise, cloves and cinnamon sticks. Bring to a boil, then lower the heat to simmer till cooked.

Serve with Nasi Kunyit (yellow rice)(page 109).

AYAM BUAH KELUAK
CHICKEN AND PORK RIBS
WITH BUAH KELUAK NUTS

- 1   chicken (1½kg) cut into serving pieces
- 200 gm pork ribs (chopped into serving pieces)
- 1   tbsp tamarind (mixed with 900mℓ water, strain liquid for use)
- ½   tbsp sugar
- 1   tsp salt
- 4   tbsps cooking oil
- 12 pieces buah keluak nuts
- 30 gm minced pork
- 1   tsp sugar
- ¼   tsp salt

Grind together:

- 3   cm length galangal
- 3   cm length tumeric
- 1   stalk lemon grass (discard outer green layer, use white portion only)
- 10 dried chillies (soaked, washed and seeded)
- 4   candlenuts
- 20 shallots
- 1   tsp shrimp paste (belachan)

Add:

- 1   tsp coriander powder
- 1   stalk lemon grass (crushed, discard outer green layer, use white portion only)

To prepare the buah keluak: Scrub each nut clean and soak in water 3 days before cooking. Change the water several times. Boil in hot water for 10 minutes before use. Make a small opening in the nut by chipping away the smooth portion of the thicker end of each nut. Scoop out the flesh from the shell and grind it into a paste. Add sugar, salt and minced pork. Mix well. Refill each hollowed nut with the meat mixture. Set aside.

To cook: Heat a saucepan till hot and pour in the oil. When the oil is hot, add the ground ingredients as well as the coriander powder and lemon grass. Stir fry the ground ingredients till fragrant. Lower the heat and add the chicken and pork ribs. Stir fry for 5 minutes. Next, add the meat-filled nuts and stir fry for a further 5 minutes. Pour in the tamarind water and bring to a boil. Add the salt and sugar. Lower the heat and simmer till the chicken is cooked and the sauce thickens.

ITEK TIM
DUCK COOKED IN SALTED MUSTARD
CABBAGE (KIAM CHYE) SOUP

- 1 duck (rubbed in ½ tbsp brandy, cut into serving pieces and rinsed)
- 500 gm pork leg or pork belly (cut into serving pieces)
- 500 gm salted mustard cabbage (soaked in water for 1 hour and rinsed before use)
- 1 piece tamarind fruit
- 4 pieces sour plum
- 6 cm length galangal (bruised)
- 6 cloves garlic (crushed)
- 3 ℓ water
- 1 tsp salt
- 1 tbsp brandy

Boil the water in a large soup pot. Add the pork leg or pork belly and boil for 10 minutes. Add the duck and bring to a boil again. Next, add the salted mustard cabbage, tamarind fruit, sour plum, galangal, garlic, salt and brandy. Simmer for an hour till the duck is tender.

ITEK CHIN
BRAISED DUCK IN SPICY SAUCE

(A):
- 1 duck (rubbed with salt, washed, drained and cut into serving pieces)
- 4 tbsps cooking oil
- 450 ml water
- ½ tsp salt
- 3 cm length ginger (bruised)

Grind together (B):
- 3 fresh red chillies
- 10 shallots
- 2 cloves garlic
- 1 tbsp soy beans

Add:
- 1 tbsp coriander powder

Marinade (C):
- 1 tbsp sugar
- 1 tbsp dark soy sauce
- 1 tbsp oyster sauce
- ½ tsp pepper
- ½ tsp salt

Marinate the duck pieces with the marinade ingredients (C). Set aside for several hours.

Heat a saucepan till hot, then add the oil. When the oil is hot, add the ground ingredients and the coriander powder. Stir fry till fragrant.

Add the duck and stir fry for a few minutes, mixing well with the ground ingredients. Pour in the water and add the ginger. Bring to a boil, then lower the heat, allowing it to simmer till the duck is tender. If the gravy thickens too much, add a little more water. Season with salt.

Shopping list:

Guest list

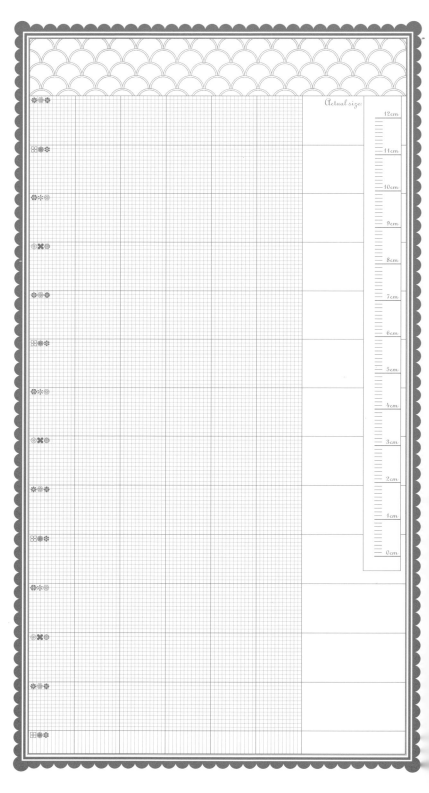

Actual size:

12cm
11cm
10cm
9cm
8cm
7cm
6cm
5cm
4cm
3cm
2cm
1cm
0cm

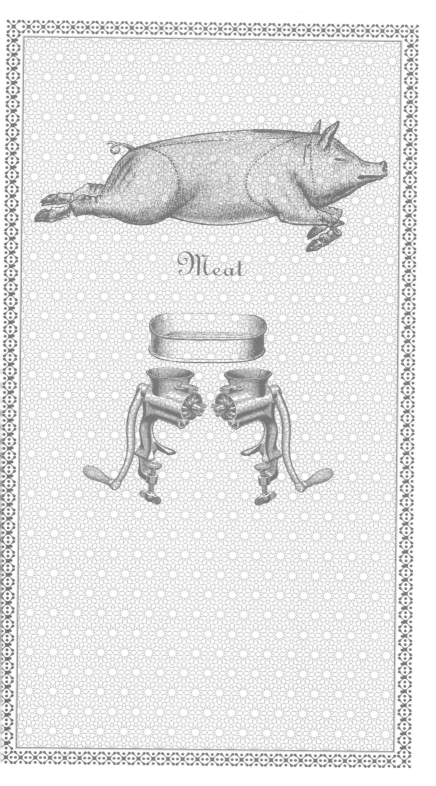

Meat

SATAY AYAM OR SATAY BABI
CHICKEN OR PORK SPICY KEBABS

(A):
- 500 gm skinned chicken breast or boneless pork loin
- 1 tbsp tamarind (mixed with 4 tbsps water, strain liquid for use) – only for chicken
- 50 satay sticks
- 4 tbsps thick coconut milk (squeeze extract from 1 grated coconut)

Grind together (B):
- 1 stalk lemon grass (discard outer green layer, use white portion only)
- 8 shallots

Add (C):
- ½ tbsp coriander powder
- 1 tsp cumin powder
- 1 tsp tumeric powder
- 1 tsp salt
- 1 tbsp brown or white sugar
- 4 tbsps cooking oil

Garnish:
cucumber (sliced)
onions (quartered)

Cut the meat into 2cm square and 1cm thick pieces. If using chicken, mix together with the tamarind water. Place ingredients (B) and (C) in a bowl. Add the meat pieces and mix well. Set aside for at least 1 hour.

Thread the satay sticks through the marinated meat pieces. Ensure that one end of each stick is completely covered by the meat. Brush the meat with coconut milk (do this just before grilling).

Grill over a charcoal fire, brushing the satay occasionally with oil. Turn the meat over several times whilst grilling.

Serve with satay sauce, cucumber slices and onions.

SAUCE FOR SATAY

- 1 tbsp tamarind (mixed with 150mℓ water, strain liquid for use)
- 3 tbsps sugar
- 1½ tsps salt
- 2 stalks lemon grass (bruised, discard outer green layer, use white portion only)
- 5 tbsps cooking oil
- 400 gm peanuts (roasted and ground)
- 400 mℓ water
- 200 mℓ coconut milk (add 100mℓ water to 1 grated coconut, squeeze mixture for coconut milk)

Grind together:
- 3 cm length galangal
- 2 candlenuts
- 10 shallots
- 4 cloves garlic
- 15 dried chillies (soaked, washed and seeded)
- 1 tsp shrimp paste (belachan)

Heat a saucepan till hot, then add the oil. When the oil is hot, add the ground ingredients and lemon grass. Stir fry the ingredients till fragrant. Add the tamarind water and bring to a boil.

Next, add the sugar, salt, ground peanuts and water. Lower the heat and simmer till the sauce thickens.

To serve: Pour sauce into individual serving bowls. Place the satay on a serving platter with sliced cucumbers, onions and ketupat (compressed rice cakes).

SATAY LEMBU OR SATAY KAMBING
BEEF OR MUTTON SPICY KEBABS

(A):
- 500 gm beef or mutton (topside)
- 1 tbsp tamarind (mixed with 4 tbsps water, strain liquid for use)
- 40 satay sticks

Grind together (B):
- 4 slices galangal
- 4 slices ginger
- 1 stalk lemon grass (discard outer green layer, use white portion only)
- 2 candlenuts
- 8 shallots
- 2 cloves garlic

Add (C):
- ½ tbsp coriander powder
- 1 tsp cumin powder
- 1 tsp tumeric powder
- 1 tsp salt
- 1½ tbsps brown sugar
- 6 tbsps cooking oil

Garnish:
cucumber (sliced)
onions (quartered)

Cut the meat into 2cm square and 1cm thick pieces. Mix with the tamarind water. Marinate the meat with ingredients (B) and (C). Mix well and set aside for at least 4 hours.

Thread the satay sticks through the marinated meat pieces. Ensure that one end of each stick is completely covered by the meat.

Grill over a charcoal fire, brushing the satay occasionally with oil. Turn the meat over several times whilst grilling.

Serve with satay sauce, cucumber slices and onions.

SATAY BABI REBUS
BOILED SPICED PORK

- 500 gm lean pork (sliced)
- 200 ml coconut milk (add 125ml water to ½ grated coconut, squeeze mixture for coconut milk)
  cucumber (sliced)

Grind together:
- 4 stalks lemon grass (discard outer green layer, use white portion only)
- 15 dried chillies (soaked, washed and seeded)
- 4 candlenuts
- 16 shallots
- 1 tsp shrimp paste (belachan)

Marinade:
- 1 tsp salt
- ½ tsp pepper
- 1 tsp sugar
- 1 tbsp cooking oil

Mix the sliced pork with the marinade ingredients, coconut milk and the ground ingredients. Set aside for at least 1 hour.

Place all the ingredients in a saucepan and bring to a boil. Lower the heat and simmer till the meat is cooked.

Serve with cucumber slices.

PENANG NONYA NGOH HIANG
PENANG STYLE PORK SOY BEAN ROLL

- 600 gm boneless pork loin
- 100 gm firm pork belly fat
- 2 tbsps spring onions (chopped)
- 3-4 water chestnuts (peeled, chopped and drained)
- 6-9 tbsps water
- 8 tbsps sweet potato flour
- 2-3 pieces of transparent dried soy bean skin (wiped clean and dried)
- 10 cups vegetable oil

Marinade:
- 6 cloves garlic (finely ground)
- 1 tbsp sugar
- ½ tsp light soy sauce
- 1 tsp salt
- 1 tsp white pepper powder
- 1 tsp Chinese 5-spice powder
- 1 tsp dark soy sauce

Garnish:
cucumber (sliced)
penang nonya chilli sauce

Trim the fat from the pork loin, leaving only the lean meat. Cut into ½cm slices lengthwise, then cut again into ½cm thick strips. Each strip should be about 8cm long. Cut the pork belly fat into similar sized strips. Place marinade in a mixing bowl and mix it with sweet potato flour and 5 tablespoons water. Stir the strips of lean pork and pork belly fat into the mixture and mix well till the mixture hardens slightly. Add the rest of the water and stir constantly till the mixture firms. Add the chopped water chestnuts and spring onions.

Cut each soy bean skin into 4 pieces. Spread out the quartered soy bean skin and lay the meat strips in one direction, lengthwise with about 8-9 strips making the length of the roll. Roll the bean skin. Leave for at least 2 hours before deep frying.

Heat a deep saucepan till hot, then add the oil for deep frying. When the oil is hot, add the ngoh hiang rolls and deep fry till golden brown and crisp. Drain off the excess oil. Slice the rolls into 2cm thick slices and serve with cucumber wedges and chilli sauce.

PENANG NONYA DEEP FRIED CHA SHAO
PENANG STYLE DEEP FRIED PORK

- 500 gm pork belly (with skin removed)
- 6-8 cups cooking oil

Marinade:
- 10 cloves garlic (finely ground)
- 1 tbsp sugar
- ½ tsp light soy sauce
- 1 tsp salt
- 1 tsp white pepper powder
- 1 tsp Chinese 5-spice powder
- 2 tsps dark soy sauce

Garnish:
cucumber (sliced)
penang nonya chilli sauce

Slice pork belly into 1cm thick pieces. Cut against the grain of the meat. Place the marinade ingredients in a mixing bowl. Add the meat and mix well. Leave aside for 2 hours.

Heat a deep saucepan till hot, then add the cooking oil. When the oil is hot, add the marinated meat and deep fry for 4-5 minutes till golden brown and crisp. Drain off the excess oil. Cut into bite-sized pieces. Serve with cucumber wedges and Penang nonya chilli sauce (below).

PENANG NONYA CHILLI SAUCE

- 1 tbsp sugar
- 1 tbsp lime juice
- 1 clove garlic (finely ground)
- ½ tsp salt
- 4 tbsps bottled sweet chilli sauce
- 2 tbsps tomato sauce (ketchup)
- 2 tbsps toasted sesame seeds
- 2 tbsps toasted peanuts (ground)

Mix the lime juice and sugar in a bowl. Ensure that the sugar dissolves. Add the remaining ingredients and stir well.

BABI PANGGANG
ROAST PORK WITH PICKLED RADISH

1 kg pork belly (in one piece with skin,
  wash and pat very dry)

Marinade (A):
4 cloves garlic (crushed)
1 tbsp salt
¼ tsp pepper

Sauce mixed together (B):
120 gm shallots (finely ground)
2 tbsps sugar
1 tbsp dark soy sauce
½ tbsp coriander powder
½ tsp Chinese 5-spice powder

Pickled radish (C):
500 gm white radish
250 gm carrots
4 tbsps sugar
  bowl of salt water
  dash of salt
  dash of vinegar

Garnish:
2 fresh red chillies (sliced and seeded)

Slice the pork belly lengthwise, 2cm apart to within 1cm of the skin so that the skin is still intact and in one piece. Marinate the meat with ingredients (A) for 2 hours. Roast it in the oven for 15 minutes under medium heat with the skin facing up. Remove the meat from the oven and prick the skin with a sharp fork. Place it under the grill until the skin crackles and turns a deep brown. Put it back in the oven for a further 20 minutes. Pour the sauce (B) onto the underside of the pork and put it into the oven for a further 25 minutes, or until the meat is cooked.

To prepare the pickled radish: Skin the carrot and radish and cut into thin strips. Soak in salt water for ½ hour, rinse and squeeze out the access water. Rub in the sugar, then add the vinegar and salt to taste.

Garnish with sliced fresh red chillies and serve with the pork.

BABI ASSAM
PORK IN TAMARIND

- 300 gm pork belly
- 2 red and 4 green chillies (slit lengthwise)
- ½ tbsp salted soy beans (tau cheo) ground
- ½ tbsp tamarind (mixed with 275mℓ water, strain liquid for use)
- 2 tbsps cooking oil
- ½ tsp salt
- 2 tsps sugar
  water

Grind together:
- 2 candlenuts
- 6 shallots
- ½ tsp shrimp paste (belachan)

Slice the pork into 2½cm slices. Sprinkle with salt and sugar and leave to marinate for 1 hour.

Heat a saucepan and when hot, add the oil. When the oil is hot, add the ground ingredients. Stir fry the ground ingredients till fragrant. Lower the heat, sprinkle a little water to prevent burning and add the ground soy beans. Stir fry for another minute.

Add the marinated pork, then sprinkle with a little more water. Next, add the salt, sugar and tamarind water. Bring to a boil and then lower the heat. Simmer till the liquid reduces by half. Add the chillies and simmer till the gravy thickens and coats the pork.

Shopping list:

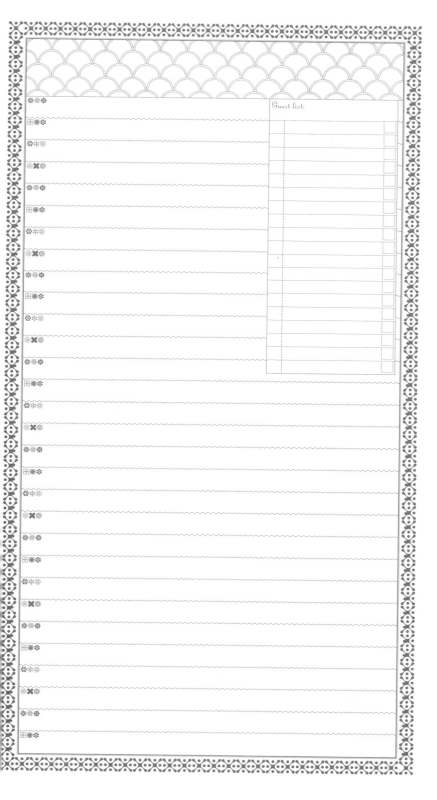

Guest list

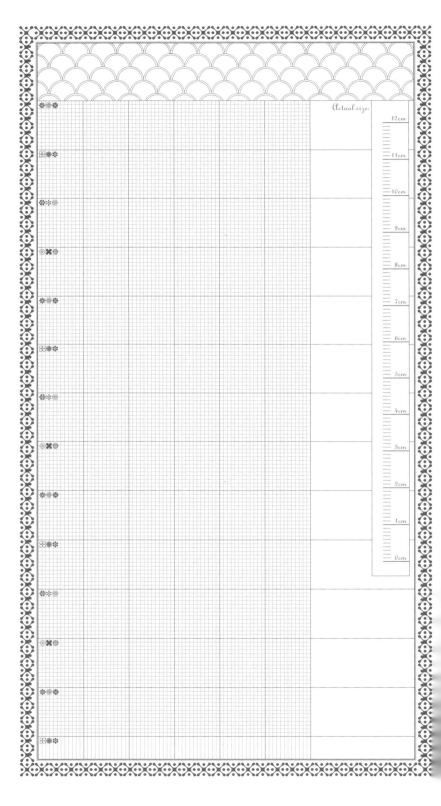

Actual size:

12cm
11cm
10cm
9cm
8cm
7cm
6cm
5cm
4cm
3cm
2cm
1cm
0cm

Seafood

ASSAM SOTONG GORENG
SQUID FRIED IN TAMARIND

300 gm small squid (pull the head off, discard the eyes and
　　bones, clean and leave the ink sac intact)
　4 tbsps cooking oil
　2 shallots (sliced)

Marinade:
　1 tbsp tamarind (mixed with 2 tbsps water,
　　strain liquid for use)
　½ tsp salt

Garnish:
　cucumber (sliced)

Marinate the squid with the tamarind water and salt. Set aside
for an hour. Drain off the excess liquid.

Heat a saucepan till hot, then add the oil. When the oil is hot,
add the shallots and stir fry for 1 minute. Add the marinated
squid and stir fry for another minute.

Remove the squid to prevent overcooking and set aside. Lower
the heat and allow the gravy in the saucepan to simmer, to reduce
and thicken till the oil breaks. Return the squid to the saucepan
and stir fry till the blackened oil covers the squid and thickens.

Serve with cucumber slices.

SAMBAL SOTONG GORENG
FRIED SPICY SQUID

- 600 gm squid
- ½ tbsp tamarind (mixed with 10 tbsps water, strain liquid for use)
- ½ small pineapple (cut into pieces)
- 1 onion (quartered)
- 1 tsp salt
- 2 tsps sugar
- 2 tbsps cooking oil

Grind together:
- 2 fresh red chillies (seeded)
- 8 dried chillies (soaked, washed and seeded)
- 3 cm length tumeric
- 10 shallots
- 2 cloves garlic

To prepare the squid: Use a knife to make a slit down the centre of each squid. Discard the eyes, bones and ink sac. Wash clean to remove the ink. Peel off the dotted membrane covering the squid. Halve each squid and make shallow criss-cross cuts across the squid. Cut each half section into 4 pieces. Marinate the squid pieces with ⅓ of the ground ingredients for at least 15 minutes.

Heat a saucepan till hot, then add the oil. When the oil is hot, add the remaining ground ingredients. Stir fry till fragrant. Add the tamarind water, salt and sugar. Simmer for a minute then add the pineapple and onions. Bring to a boil for 2 minutes. Lower the heat and simmer till the pineapple is soft. Add the squid and cook, covered, for 2 minutes. Remove the cover to stir occasionally. Be careful not to overcook the squid.

SAMBAL SOTONG SUMBAT
SQUID SAMBAL WITH MEAT
AND PRAWN STUFFING

- 300 gm medium sized squid
- ½ tbsp tamarind (mixed with 100ml water, strain liquid for use)
- 120 ml coconut milk (add 100ml water to ¼ grated coconut, squeeze mixture for coconut milk)
- 1 stalk lemon grass (bruised, discard outer green layer, use white portion only)
- ½ tsp salt
- ½ tsp sugar
- 2 tbsps cooking oil
- toothpicks

Stuffing:
- 200 gm minced pork or beef
- 150 gm minced prawn
- ¼ tsp salt
- ¼ tsp pepper

Grind together:
- 8 shallots
- 4 dried chillies (soaked, washed and seeded)
- 2 fresh red chillies
- 2 candlenuts
- 2 slices galangal
- 2 slices tumeric
- 1 tsp shrimp paste (belachan)

To prepare the squid: Pull the head off the squid. Discard the eyes, bones and ink sac but retain the head. Wash the squid to remove the ink. Drain dry.

Mix the stuffing ingredients well. Stuff this meat mixture into each squid. Re-attach the squid head with the help of a toothpick.

Heat the saucepan till hot and add the oil. When the oil is hot, add the ground ingredients and lemon grass. Stir fry till fragrant. Add the tamarind water. Stir fry for another minute. Add the coconut milk, salt and sugar. When the gravy boils, add the stuffed squid. Lower the heat to simmer for a further 10 minutes till the squid is cooked.

ASSAM UDANG GORENG
PRAWNS FRIED IN TAMARIND

- 300 gm large prawns
-   3 tbsps cooking oil

Marinade:
- 1 tbsp tamarind (mixed with 2 tbsps water, strain liquid for use)
- 2 tbsps water
- ½ tsp salt
- ½ tsp sugar
- ½ tsp pepper

Garnish:
cucumber (sliced)

To prepare the prawns: Trim the sharp ends of the feelers and legs of each prawn. Split the back of the prawns and remove the black intestinal veins. Wash thoroughly.

Place the prawns in the marinade for 1 hour. Drain off the liquid completely.

Heat the saucepan over high heat and add the oil. When it is hot, add the prawns and stir fry for 1 minute. Lower the heat. Stir fry the prawns further till they are cooked and the shells crisp.

Serve with cucumber slices.

GULAI LEMAK NANAS
PINEAPPLE CURRY WITH PRAWNS

- 300 gm medium sized prawns (shelled and cleaned)
- 500 ml thick coconut milk (add 450ml water to ½ grated coconut, squeeze mixture for thick coconut milk)
- 950 ml thin coconut milk (add 900ml water to the same ½ grated coconut, squeeze mixture for thin coconut milk)
- 1 small pineapple (skinned, remove the core, cut into quarters and then triangular slices)
- ½ tsp salt
- 1 tbsp coriander powder

Grind together:
- 1 stalk lemon grass (discard outer green layer, use white portion only)
- 5 shallots
- 3 cloves garlic
- 3 cm length tumeric
- 5 dried chillies (soaked, washed and seeded)
- 4 fresh red chillies
- ½ tsp shrimp paste (belachan)

Heat a saucepan till hot, then add the oil. When the oil is hot, add the ground ingredients and the coriander powder.

Stir fry the ground ingredients till fragrant. Pour in half the thin coconut milk a little at a time.

Bring to a boil then add the pineapple pieces. Cook for a minute, then add the remaining thin coconut milk and cook till the pineapple pieces soften. Add the prawns and salt. Pour in the thick coconut milk and simmer for about 20 minutes or till the oil breaks.

SAMBAL UDANG
PRAWNS IN THICK AND SPICY SAUCE

- 300 gm medium sized prawns
  (shelled and cleaned)
- 1 tsp tamarind (mixed with 2 tbsps water,
  strain liquid for use)
- ½ tsp salt
- 1 tsp sugar
- 4 tbsps oil

Grind together:
- 10 dried chillies (soaked, washed and seeded)
- 3 candlenuts
- 15 shallots
- ½ tsp shrimp paste (belachan)

Heat a saucepan till hot, then add the oil. When it is hot, add the ground ingredients and stir fry for 1 minute. Over high heat, stir in the prawns and stir fry for another minute.

Reduce the heat and add the tamarind water, sugar and salt. Stir fry till the prawns are cooked and the oil separates.

UDANG GARAM ASSAM
PRAWNS COOKED IN TAMARIND GRAVY

     500 gm large prawns
      ½ tbsp tamarind (mixed with 450mℓ water,
          strain liquid for use)
      1 stalk lemon grass (bruised, discard outer green layer,
          use white portion only)
      1 tsp sugar
      ½ tsp salt
      2 tbsps cooking oil

      Grind together:
      6 dried chillies (soaked, washed and seeded)
      6 slices galangal
      3 cm length tumeric
      3 candlenuts
     12 shallots
      1 tsp shrimp paste (belachan)

To prepare the prawns: Trim the sharp ends of the feelers and legs of each prawn. Split the back of the prawns and remove the black intestinal vein. Wash thoroughly.

Heat a saucepan till hot, then add the oil. When it is hot, add the ground ingredients and stir fry for 2 minutes. Lower the heat and continue to stir fry the ground ingredients till fragrant.

Add ¼ of the tamarind water and the bruised lemon grass. Stir fry for another 2 minutes.

Pour in the remaining tamarind water, sugar and salt. Bring to a boil. Add the prawns and bring to a boil again. Lower the heat and simmer uncovered for about 10 minutes, or until the prawns are cooked.

UDANG GORENG CHILLI
FRIED PRAWNS IN CHILLI

- 500 gm large prawns
- 1 tsp salt
- 3 tbsps oil

Grind together:
- 12 fresh red chillies (seeded)
- 8 cloves garlic
- 2 shallots

To prepare the prawns: Trim the sharp ends of the feelers and legs of each prawn. Split the back of the prawns and remove the black intestinal vein. Wash thoroughly.

Heat the saucepan and add the oil. When the oil is hot, stir fry the ground ingredients till fragrant and the oil floats. Add the prawns, then the salt to taste. Stir fry till cooked.

UDANG GORENG
DEEP FRIED GOLDEN PRAWNS

(A):

12	pieces large prawns
150	gm fish paste
100	gm minced pork
4	tbsps corn flour
1	egg (lightly beaten)
4	tbsps plain flour
	bread crumbs
	oil for deep frying

Marinade for prawns (B):

2	slices ginger
½	stalk spring onion
¼	tsp pepper
¼	tsp salt

Marinade for fish paste and minced pork (C):

1	tsp chilli powder
½	tsp salt
½	tsp sugar
1	tsp corn flour
1	tsp sesame oil

Garnish:
cucumber (sliced)
chilli sauce

Shell the prawns, discard the heads and leave the tails intact. Slit the back of the prawns to remove the intestinal vein, taking care not to split the prawns. Marinate the prawns with (B). Set aside. Combine the minced pork and fish paste and marinate with (C). Knead thoroughly and divide it into 12 equal portions.

Coat the prawns with a layer of corn flour, then place one portion of the meat mixture into the back slit of each prawn. Coat it with another layer of plain flour. Dip each prawn into the beaten egg and roll it in the bread crumbs. Refrigerate for an hour. Heat the oil in a saucepan till hot. Deep fry the coated prawns at medium heat until golden brown. Remove and drain off the excess oil.

Serve with cucumber wedges and chilli sauce.

UDANG PEDAS NANAS
PRAWNS AND PINEAPPLE IN SPICY GRAVY

- 600 gm large prawns
- 1 small pineapple
- 1 ℓ water
- 1 tsp salt
- 1 tsp sugar

Grind together:
- 8 slices galangal
- 3 cm length tumeric
- 14 shallots
- 4 fresh red chillies (seeded)
- 1 tsp shrimp paste (belachan)

To prepare the prawns: Trim the sharp ends of the feelers and legs of each prawn. Split the back of the prawns and remove the black intestinal vein. Wash thoroughly.

To prepare the pineapple: Remove the outer skin and eyes of the pineapple. Core the pineapple and cut into cubes.

To cook: Place the ground ingredients and pineapple cubes into a pot with 1ℓ of water. Bring to a boil.

Simmer for 10 minutes, before adding the prawns. Boil till the prawns are cooked.

Season with salt and sugar.

SAMBAL UDANG KERING
DRIED PRAWN FLOSS

    300 gm dried prawns (washed and finely ground)
      1 tsp tamarind (mixed with 2 tbsps water,
        strain liquid for use)
      4 tbsps cooking oil
      5 pieces lime leaves (optional)
      1 tbsp sugar (or to taste)

      Grind together:
      4 red chillies (seeded)
      3 candlenuts
      1 stalk lemon grass (discard outer green layer,
        use white portion only)
      8 shallots
      2 thin slices galangal
      2 thin slices tumeric

Heat a saucepan till hot, then add the oil. When the oil is hot,
lower the heat and stir fry the ground ingredients till fragrant.
Pour in the tamarind water and allow it to simmer, stirring
continuously.

Add the ground dried prawns, lime leaves and sugar. Simmer
over moderate heat, stirring continuously till the mixture dries
and becomes crisp. This takes approximately 30 minutes.

This dish can be served with Nasi Lemak (page 108) or used as
a sandwich filling.

IKAN CURRY
FISH CURRY

- 500 gm red snapper or Spanish mackerel (ikan tenggiri)
  cut into pieces
- 250 gm lady's fingers (okra) or aubergines (brinjals)
  cut and parboiled
- 5 green chillies (slit lengthwise)
- 2 tomatoes (quartered)
- 3 cm length ginger (cut into strips)
- 4 shallots (sliced)
- 4 cloves garlic (sliced)
- 1½ tbsps curry powder (mixed with 2 tbsps water
  to form a paste)
- 500 ml coconut milk (add 450ml water to ¼ grated coconut,
  squeeze mixture for coconut milk)
- 2 tsps tamarind (mixed with 200ml water,
  strain liquid for use)
- ½ tsp salt
- ½ tsp sugar
- 4 tbsps cooking oil

Heat a saucepan. When it is hot, add the oil. When the oil is hot, stir fry the garlic, then add the shallots and ginger. Stir fry the ingredients till golden brown.

Add 2 tablespoons coconut milk, then the curry paste. Lower the heat and stir fry the ingredients till the oil breaks and comes to the surface. Add the remaining coconut milk and simmer for a while before adding the tamarind water, salt and sugar.

Cook for 2 minutes, then add the fish and the lady's fingers, green chillies and tomato. Simmer over low heat till cooked.

GULAI IKAN ASSAM
HOT AND SOUR FISH STEW

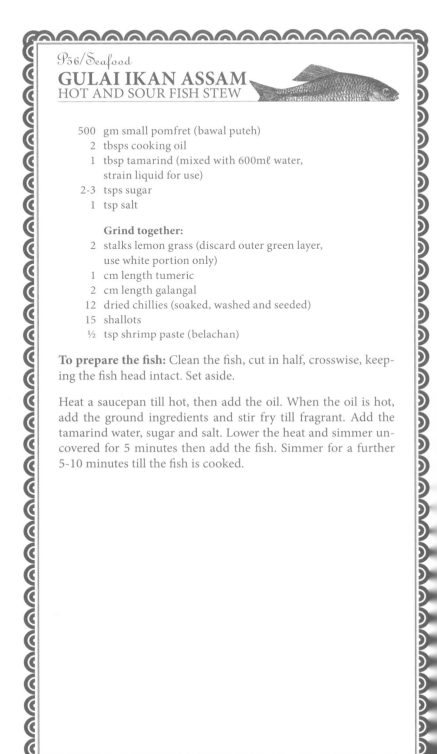

- 500 gm small pomfret (bawal puteh)
- 2 tbsps cooking oil
- 1 tbsp tamarind (mixed with 600ml water, strain liquid for use)
- 2-3 tsps sugar
- 1 tsp salt

Grind together:
- 2 stalks lemon grass (discard outer green layer, use white portion only)
- 1 cm length tumeric
- 2 cm length galangal
- 12 dried chillies (soaked, washed and seeded)
- 15 shallots
- ½ tsp shrimp paste (belachan)

To prepare the fish: Clean the fish, cut in half, crosswise, keeping the fish head intact. Set aside.

Heat a saucepan till hot, then add the oil. When the oil is hot, add the ground ingredients and stir fry till fragrant. Add the tamarind water, sugar and salt. Lower the heat and simmer uncovered for 5 minutes then add the fish. Simmer for a further 5-10 minutes till the fish is cooked.

IKAN GULAI PENANG
PENANG STYLE FISH

- 600 gm red snapper or Spanish mackerel (ikan tenggiri)
- 300 gm lady's fingers (okra) discard stem and cut into pieces
- 6 stalks laksa leaves (discard stem)
- 1 tsp tamarind (mixed with 450mℓ water, strain liquid for use)
- 1 tsp sugar
- ½ tsp salt
- 2 tbsps cooking oil

Grind together:
- 1 stalk lemon grass (discard outer green layer, use white portion only)
- 3 cm length tumeric
- 15 dried chillies (soaked, washed and seeded)
- 1 clove garlic
- 15 shallots
- 1 tsp shrimp paste (belachan)

Heat a saucepan till hot, then add the oil. When the oil is hot, add the ground ingredients.

Stir fry the ingredients till fragrant. Add the salt and sugar. Next, pour in the tamarind water and bring to a boil. Add the lady's fingers, lower the heat and simmer for a while. Lastly, add the fish and laksa leaves. Simmer till cooked.

KUAH LADAH
FISH COOKED IN TAMARIND
AND PEPPER GRAVY

- 600 gm ray fish, cut into pieces
-    3 aubergines (brinjals) cut into 4 strips lengthwise,
      then crosswise about 5cm wide and soaked in salt water
-    1 tbsp tamarind (mixed with ½ℓ water,
      strain liquid for use)
-   ½ tsp salt
-   ½ tsp sugar
-    3 tbsps cooking oil

Grind together:
-    1 tsp peppercorns or pepper powder
-    8 slices galangal
-    3 cm length tumeric
-    3 candlenuts
-   12 shallots
-    2 cloves garlic
-    1 tsp shrimp paste (belachan)

Heat a saucepan till hot, then add the oil. When the oil is hot, add the ground ingredients.

Stir fry for 1-2 minutes. Sprinkle with a little tamarind water and continue to stir fry till fragrant.

Sprinkle more of the tamarind water and add the pieces of aubergines. Pour in the remaining tamarind water. Add the salt and sugar. Lastly, add the fish and bring to a boil. Then lower the heat and simmer about 10 minutes or till cooked.

OTAK OTAK
SPICY FISH WRAPPED IN BANANA LEAF

(A):
- 500 gm minced fish meat
- 150 mℓ coconut milk (add 50mℓ water to 1 grated coconut, squeeze mixture for coconut milk)
- 2 eggs
  cooking oil
  banana leaves
  toothpicks

Grind together (B):
- 3 cm length galangal
- 6 cm length tumeric
- 2 stalks lemon grass (discard outer green layer, use white portion only)
- 5 candlenuts
- 15 dried chillies (soaked, washed and seeded)
- 20 shallots
- 1 tsp shrimp paste (belachan)

Add (C):
- 1 tbsp coriander powder
- ½ tbsp sugar
- ¼ tsp salt

Heat the saucepan till hot, then add the oil. When the oil is hot, add the ground ingredients (B). Stir fry till fragrant. Add ingredients (C) and stir fry till fragrant and the oil breaks. Set aside to cool.

After it has cooled, add the fish meat and coconut milk (A). Mix well. Separate into about 20 portions and use the banana leaves to wrap each portion of the fish mixture in rectangular blocks. Use toothpicks to keep the banana leaves in place.

Grill each banana leaf wrapped fish on charcoal, or in the oven for 15 minutes or till cooked.

SAMBAL LENGKONG
FISH FLOSS

    600 gm fish (ikan parang, cut into small pieces)
    300 ml coconut milk (add 200ml water to ¾ grated coconut,
            squeeze mixture for coconut milk)
     ½ tsp salt
     2 tbsps sugar
     ½ tbsp lime juice

Grind together:
     8 dried chillies (soaked, washed and seeded)
     2 slices tumeric
     2 slices galangal
    10 shallots
     4 candlenuts
     1 stalk lemon grass (discard outer green layer,
         use white portion only)
     ½ tsp shrimp paste (belachan)

Heat a saucepan till hot. Add the ground ingredients, sugar, lime juice and salt. Pour in the coconut milk. Bring to a boil. Lower the heat, add the fish and simmer till cooked. Remove the fish and flake the fish meat.

Allow the remaining gravy to continue boiling to reduce by half. Add the flaked fish and cook for an hour, stirring continuously till the fish is dry and crisp.

Cool on greaseproof paper and keep in an airtight container. This dish can be used as a sandwich filling.

Shopping list:

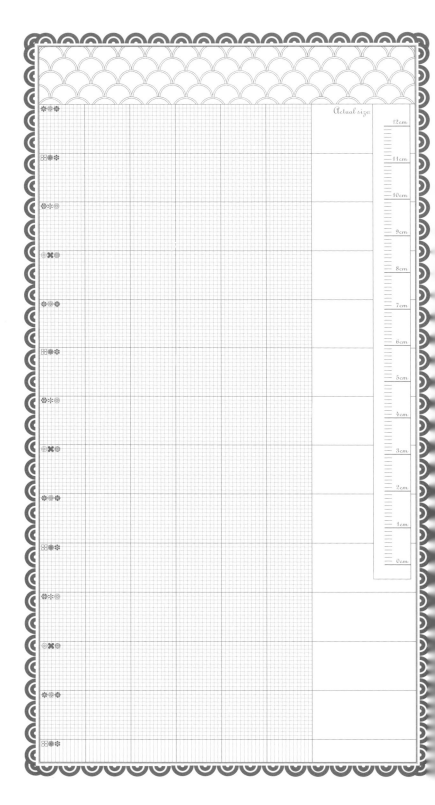

Actual size:

12cm

11cm

10cm

9cm

8cm

7cm

6cm

5cm

4cm

3cm

2cm

1cm

0cm

Vegetables

CHAP CHYE
CABBAGE FRIED WITH DRIED CHINESE INGREDIENTS

- 250 gm pork belly (rinsed then boiled till it softens and cut into thin slices)
- 250 gm small prawns (shelled and cleaned) save the shells for stock
- 250 gm cabbage (cut into small square pieces)
- 1 tbsp salted soy beans (tau cheo) ground
- 1 tsp salt
- 4 tbsps oil
  water

Dried ingredients:
- 30 gm lily flowers (kim chiam)
- 15 gm black jelly fungus or cloud's ears (bok gee)
- 10 gm black Chinese mushroom
- 2 pieces beancurd sticks (tau kee)
- 10 gm glass noodles (tung hoon)

Grind together:
- 4 candlenuts
- 2 cloves garlic
- 12 shallots

Prawn Stock: Boil the prawn shells in 1ℓ of water. Strain the liquid for use.

Preparation of dried ingredients: Rinse the dried ingredients well. Soak for 30 minutes to soften (except for the beancurd sticks). Lily flowers – cut off both hard ends. Knot into pairs. Black jelly fungus – cut into 2, soak in water, taking care to remove the grid. Black Chinese mushroom – remove the stumps, cut into quarters and soak in water. Beancurd sticks – break into 6cm length pieces before soaking in water. Glass noodles – cut to a shorter length.

Heat the saucepan till it is very hot. Add the oil. Stir fry the ground ingredients and sprinkle it with a little water to prevent burning. Add the salted soy beans and stir fry for a minute. Next, add the pork belly and prawns. Sprinkle with a little more water. Add the cabbage, lily flowers, black fungus, beancurd sticks and mushroom.

Cook for a few minutes before adding the prawn stock and salt. Bring to a boil again and then simmer till the vegetables soften. Add the glass noodles and simmer for a further 5 minutes.

FRIED KIAM CHYE
FRIED PRESERVED MUSTARD CABBAGE WITH BELLY PORK

- 250 gm preserved mustard cabbage (kiam chye)
- 150 gm pork belly
- 2 fresh red chillies (sliced)
- ½ tbsp sugar
- ¼ tbsp dark soy sauce
- 2 cloves garlic (minced)
- 2 tbsps cooking oil

To prepare ingredients: Soak the preserved mustard cabbage in water for 1 hour. This is to remove the excess salt. Squeeze it dry and shred the vegetables finely.

Boil the pork belly in water till soft. Slice into pieces ½cm thick.

To cook: Heat the saucepan till hot, then add the oil. When the oil is hot, add the garlic and stir fry till golden brown. Add the sliced pork belly and stir fry over high heat for a further 2 minutes.

Add the preserved mustard cabbage and stir fry for a minute before adding the sugar, dark soy sauce and sliced red chillies. Stir fry till the vegetables are soft and cooked.

GADO GADO
VEGETABLE SALAD WITH HOT PEANUT SAUCE

(A):

- 4 pieces firm beancurd cakes (tau kwa) cut into ½ then sliced)
- 10 shallots (finely sliced and deep fried)
- 10 pieces prawn crackers (fried)
- 1 cucumber (cut crosswise)
- 100 gm lettuce
- 4 eggs (hard boiled and sliced)
- 200 gm potatoes (boiled and sliced)
- 1 tbsp oil

Vegetables (B):

- 250 gm bean sprouts (parboiled and drained dry)
- 300 gm cabbage (parboiled and cut into square pieces)
- 300 gm kangkong (water convoluvous) parboiled and cut into 2½cm length
- 100 gm long beans (parboiled and cut into 2½cm length pieces)

Peanut Sauce (C):

- 300 gm peanuts (roasted and ground)
- 600 ml coconut milk (add 500ml water to ½ grated coconut, squeeze mixture for coconut milk)
- 1 tsp salt
- 8 tbsps sugar
- 2 tbsps vinegar (or 2 tbsps tamarind mixed with 200ml water, strain liquid for use)

Grind together (D):

- 20 dried chillies (soaked, washed and seeded)
- 10 shallots
- 2 cloves garlic
- 1 tsp shrimp paste (belachan)

Heat a saucepan till hot, then add the oil. When the oil is hot, add the ground ingredients (D). Stir fry for 3 minutes or till fragrant. Add the tamarind water. Stir fry for 1 minute.

Pour in the coconut milk a little at a time and bring to a boil before adding the ground peanuts. Add the salt and sugar. Lower the heat and simmer uncovered over medium heat until the oil breaks and comes to the surface. This takes about 10 minutes.

To serve: Arrange the lettuce on individual serving dishes. Pile the rest of the vegetables (B) and the sliced cucumber, on the lettuce. Next, add the sliced eggs and potatoes. Top with the fried soy bean cake pieces. Just before serving, pour the peanut sauce over and garnish with the fried prawn crackers and shallots.

SAMBAL TERONG BENDI
LADY'S FINGER SALAD

300 gm lady's fingers (okra)

Seasoning:
2 tbsps sugar
1 tbsp vinegar
2 tbsps lime juice
½ tsp salt

Grind together:
50 gm dried prawns (soaked in warm water to soften)
3 fresh red chillies (seeded)
½ tbsp toasted shrimp paste (belachan)

Garnish:
Chinese parsley

Place the lady's fingers in a pot of boiling water and boil uncovered for 3 minutes or till the colour changes. Drain and rinse in cold water. Trim the stalks of the lady's fingers and arrange them neatly on a plate.

Next, place the ground ingredients and the seasoning in a mixing bowl. Stir and mix well. Spread it over the cooked lady's fingers. Garnish with Chinese parsley.

SAMBAL TAU KWA
BEANCURD IN SPICY COCONUT MILK

- 6 pieces firm beancurd cakes (tau kwa) cut into cubes
- 3 tbsps oil
- 250 gm prawns (shelled and cleaned)
- 1 tsp salt
- 2 pieces lime leaves

Coconut milk:
- 100 ml thick coconut milk (add 50ml water to 1 grated coconut, squeeze mixture for thick coconut milk)
- 200 ml thin coconut milk (add 100ml water to the same 1 grated coconut, squeeze mixture for thin coconut milk)

Grind together:
- 1 stalk lemon grass (discard outer green layer, use white portion only)
- 1 cm length galangal
- 6-8 fresh red chillies
- 10-12 shallots
- 1 tsp dried shrimp paste (belachan)

Heat a saucepan till hot and add the oil. Lightly fry the beancurd cubes. Remove from the saucepan and set aside.

Next, stir fry the ground ingredients for 3 minutes or until fragrant. Add the prawns and stir fry for a further few minutes. Add the salt and pour in the thin coconut milk a little at a time. Bring to a slow boil, stirring continuously. Lower the heat and simmer for 1-2 minutes.

Add the beancurd cubes and lime leaves. Simmer for a further 10 minutes. Next, pour in the thick coconut milk and simmer till the gravy thickens.

TAU KWA GORENG
FRIED BEANCURD CAKES

- 4 pieces firm beancurd cakes (tau kwa)
- 150 gm bean sprouts (parboiled and drained dry)
- 1 cucumber (sliced)

Sauce, grind together:
- 5 fresh red chillies
- 3 cloves garlic

Add:
- 2 tbsps brown sugar or palm sugar
- 1 tsp vinegar (or 1 tbsp tamarind mixed with 1 tbsp water, strain liquid for use)
- 2 tbsps dark soy sauce
- ¼ tsp salt
- ½ cup peanuts (roasted and ground)

Heat a saucepan till hot. Add some oil for deep frying. When the oil is hot, deep fry the beancurd cakes till they brown lightly. Remove and cut into 3cm square pieces.

Place all the ingredients for the sauce in a mixing bowl. Mix well.

To serve: Place the fried soy bean cake pieces on serving dishes. Top with sliced cucumber and bean sprouts. Pour the peanut sauce over the salad.

SAMBAL TIMUN
SPICY CUCUMBER SALAD

(A):

2 cucumbers (skinned and cut each lengthwise into 4. Discard middle seeded portion. Slice crosswise)

200 gm pork belly (rinsed then boiled till it softens and cut into thin slices)

Grind together (B):

2 fresh red chillies (seeded)

1 tsp toasted shrimp paste (belachan)

2 tbsps dried shrimp (washed with warm water)

Add (C):

1 tbsp sugar

2 tbsps lime juice

½ tbsp vinegar

¼ tsp salt

Garnish:

4 stalks Chinese celery (use the leaves only)

Pour ingredients (C) into a mixing bowl. Mix well with a large spoon. Stir in ingredients (B). Thereafter, add ingredients (A). Mix well.

Serve in a plate dressed with the Chinese celery.

KUEH PIE TEE
PIE TEE SHELLS

130	gm corn flour
1	tbsp plain flour
200	mℓ water
1	egg (lightly beaten)
¼	tsp salt
¼	tsp pepper
	cooking oil
	pie tee mould

Put the corn flour, plain flour, salt and pepper in a mixing bowl. Add the beaten egg to the flour mixture, stirring it in gradually and slowly adding water to make a smooth batter.

Pour cooking oil into a small deep saucepan enough to fully cover the mould. Heat the oil till it is hot. Heat the pie tee mould in the hot oil. Next, dip it into the batter till it forms a thin film over the mould. Dip it into the hot oil till the pie tee shell turns slightly brown and loosens from the mould. Remove the mould from the oil and shake off the pie tee. Drain off the excess oil with paper towels. Repeat this process till all the batter is used. This recipe makes about 50 pie tee shells.

When the pie tee shells have cooled slightly, store in an air tight container to keep the shells crisp.

PIE TEE FILLING

(A):
- 600 gm bamboo shoots (finely shredded)
- 200 gm Chinese sweet turnip (bangkwang) (finely shredded)
- 300 gm prawns (shelled and diced)
- 300 gm pork (boiled and finely shredded)
- 2 pieces beancurd cakes (tau kwa) fried and shredded
- 6 cloves garlic (chopped)
- 1 tsp salted soy beans (tau cheo) ground
- ½ ℓ soup stock (from the boiled pork)
- ¼ tsp salt
- 2 tbsps cooking oil

Garnish (B):
- 100 gm cooked crab meat (shredded)
- 2 eggs (fried into an omelette and finely diced)
  coriander leaves (coarsely chopped)

Chilli and vinegar sauce (C):
- 4 fresh red chillies (ground)
- 2 tbsps vinegar
- 2 tsps water
- ¼ tsp salt
- ½ tsp sugar

Heat a saucepan till hot and add the oil. When the oil is hot, add the garlic and stir fry till golden brown. Next, add the salted soy beans (tau cheo), sprinkling a little water to prevent burning.

Add the shredded pork and the diced prawns. Stir fry till cooked, then add a little stock and some salt. Stir in the shredded bamboo shoots and add more soup stock. Leave to boil for a few minutes, before adding the shredded Chinese turnip. Cook till soft.

Lastly, add the shredded fried beancurd cakes and stir well. Simmer till cooked and the mixture is almost dry.

Prepare the sauce. Mix all the ingredients together (C).

To serve: Fill each pie tee shell with this meat and vegetable filling. Decorate the top of each filled shell with a little crab meat, omelette and coriander leaves. Serve with the freshly prepared chilli and vinegar sauce (C).

ACHAR WITH REMPAH
PICKLED VEGETABLES IN HOT,
SWEET AND SOUR SAUCE

2	kg cucumber (Discard middle seeded portion. Cut into 5cm long pieces, rub in salt, set aside for 1 hour and squeeze out the liquid)
300	gm cauliflower (cut into small pieces)
300	gm cabbage (cut into small square pieces)
150	gm carrots (cut into thin strips of 5cm length)
120	mℓ vinegar
220	gm sugar
1	tsp salt
4	tbsps cooking oil

Dressing:

2	tbsps sesame seed (fried or roasted till golden brown)
160	gm peanuts (roasted and finely ground)

Mixture for scalding the vegetables (A):

250	mℓ vinegar
125	mℓ water
1	tbsp sugar
½	tbsp salt

Grind together (B):

12	cm length tumeric
5	candlenuts
2	cloves garlic
15	dried chillies (soaked, washed and seeded)
8	shallots

Scalding the cut vegetables: Bring the mixture (A) to a boil in a saucepan. Scald each type of vegetable separately by stirring it into the mixture for 1-2 minutes, then remove the vegetables from the mixture with a perforated ladle and drain off the liquid. Place on a large tray to cool. Bring the mixture (A) to a boil again before adding the next lot of vegetables.

After all the vegetables have been scalded, discard the mixture. When the scalded vegetables have cooled, squeeze out the excess liquid. Set aside.

Heat a saucepan till hot, and add the cooking oil. Stir fry the ground ingredients (B) till fragrant then add the vinegar, salt and sugar. Set aside to cool.

To serve: Place the scalded vegetables in a big glass bowl, together with the fried ground ingredients. Mix well. Next, stir in the ground peanuts and roasted sesame seeds.

Shopping list:

Guest list:

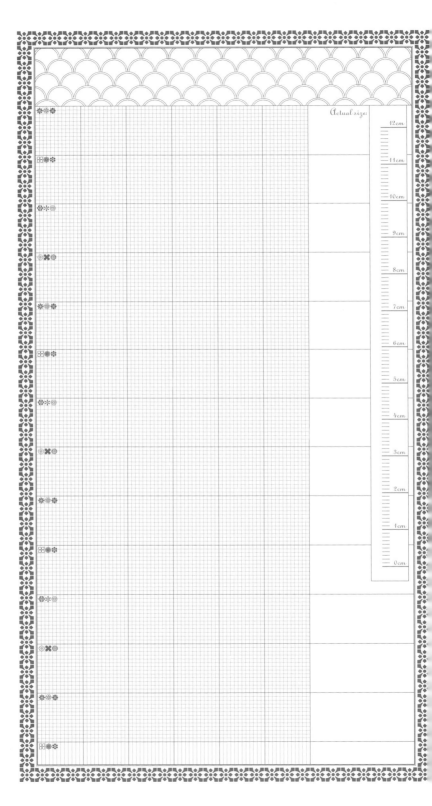

Actual size:

12cm
11cm
10cm
9cm
8cm
7cm
6cm
5cm
4cm
3cm
2cm
1cm
0cm

IKAN MASAK LEMAK KUNING
MACKERAL COOKED IN COCONUT GRAVY

- 5 pieces mackerel fish (100gm each piece)
- 1.35 ℓ coconut milk (add 1.2ℓ water to 1 grated coconut, squeeze mixture for coconut milk)
- 1 big onion (sliced)
- 1 stalk lemon grass (bruised, discard outer green layer, use white portion only)
- 4 pieces tamarind fruit
- 1 piece tumeric leaf
- 1 lime (squeezed for juice)
- ½ tsp salt

   Grind together:
- 3 cm length galangal
- 3 cm length ginger
- 4 fresh red chillies (seeded)
- 5 shallots
- 2 cloves garlic

Wash and clean the fish with lime juice to get rid of the fishy smell. Place all the ingredients (except the fish) in a pot of hot water and bring to a boil over medium heat.

Stir continuously and do not let the oil from the coconut milk break at the surface. Add the fish and simmer uncovered till the fish is cooked.

IKAN GORENG BERLADA
FRIED FISH IN CHILLI

- 500 gm fish (mackerel cut into pieces)
- 5 shallots (coarsely sliced)
- 5 fresh red chillies (ground)
- 2 tomatoes (skinned and scrapped)
- 1 lime (squeezed for juice)
- ½ tsp salt
- 10 tbsps cooking oil

Wash and clean the fish with lime juice to get rid of the fishy smell. Pat dry.

Heat a saucepan till hot. Pour in enough oil to fry the fish. When the oil is sizzling hot, lower the heat and fry the fish till golden brown. Remove the fish from the saucepan and drain off the excess oil.

Pour away most of the cooking oil from the saucepan, leaving about 2 tablespoons in the pan. Stir fry the shallots in this oil till soft, then add the tomatoes, ground chilli and salt.

Cook for 5 to 10 minutes, or till fragrant. When it is cooked, spread it on the fried fish and serve.

IKAN BAKAR
GRILLED FISH

- 6 pieces horse mackeral (kembong fish), about 100gm each
- 2 stalks lemon grass (bruised, discard outer green layer, use white portion only)
- 1 lime (squeezed for juice)
- 125 ml coconut milk (squeeze extract from ½ grated coconut and add a little of the dregs – hampas)
- ½ tsp salt

Grind together (A):
- 3 shallots
- 2 cloves garlic
- 2 cm length ginger
- 2 cm length tumeric

Chilli sauce (B):
- 1 big onion (sliced)
- 2 fresh green and 2 fresh red chillies (sliced)
- 2 limes (squeezed for juice)
- 2 tbsps dark soy sauce

Wash and clean the fish with lime juice to get rid of the fishy smell. Pat dry.

Prepare the marinade by adding the ground ingredients (A) to the coconut milk and salt. Mix well.

Tie 2 stalks of lemon grass together and use it to brush the fish with the prepared marinade. Brush both sides of the fish. Grill the fish over low heat, in the oven or over a charcoal fire. Continuously brush the fish with the marinade till it has absorbed all of it. Bake till the fish is cooked and turns golden brown.

Mix all the chilli sauce ingredients (B) together.

Serve the fish with the chilli sauce.

IKAN GULAI
FISH COOKED WITH LAKSA LEAVES

- 5   slices red snapper (100gm each)
- 200 gm lady's fingers (okra) cut off the stump at the end
- 4   stalks laksa leaves (discard stem)
- 1   tsp tamarind (mixed with 450mℓ water, strain liquid for use)
- 1   tsp sugar
- ½ tsp salt
- 2   tbsps oil

Grind together:

- 1   stalk lemon grass (discard outer green layer, use white portion only)
- 3   cm length tumeric
- 12 dried chillies (soaked, washed and seeded)
- 1   clove garlic
- 12 shallots
- 1   tsp shrimp paste (belachan)

Heat the saucepan till hot. Add the oil and when hot, lower the heat and stir fry the ground ingredients till fragrant. Add the salt, sugar and tamarind water and bring to a boil.

Add the lady's fingers and simmer for a while before putting in the fish and laksa leaves. Simmer till cooked.

IKAN MASAK LEMAK MERAH
FISH COOKED IN COCONUT GRAVY

5 pieces Spanish mackerel (ikan tenggiri) (100gm each) washed and pat dry

900 mℓ coconut milk (add 750mℓ water to 1 grated coconut, squeeze mixture for coconut milk)

100 gm long beans (washed and cut into 5cm length pieces)

1 stalk lemon grass (bruised, discard outer green layer, use white portion only)

6 cm length galangal

4 pieces tamarind fruit

1 piece tumeric leaf

½ tsp salt

Grind together:

3 cloves garlic

3 cm length ginger

3 cm length tumeric

6 fresh red chillies (seeded)

6 shallots

Place all the ground ingredients and the coconut milk in a pot and bring to a boil over medium heat. Add all the remaining ingredients (except the fish) stirring continuously to obtain a smooth textured gravy. Add the fish. Simmer uncovered, till cooked.

IKAN FRIKKADELS
FISH CUTLETS

(A):

500	gm	Spanish mackerel steamed, boned and mashed
250	gm	potatoes (boiled and smoothly mashed)
1	tsp	butter (slightly creamed)
½	tsp	salt
¼	tsp	sugar
½	tsp	pepper
1		egg yolk (beaten)
3	tsps	tapioca flour or corn flour
1		stalk spring onion (chopped)

(B):

2		egg whites (slightly beaten)
10	tbsp	oil

Garnish:
cucumber (sliced)

Combine all the ingredients (A) in a mixing bowl. Form a dough-like texture. Shape the mixture into small balls (the size of ping pong balls) and flatten it slightly to form cutlets. Dip the cutlets into the beaten egg white and deep fry in hot oil till a light golden brown.

Remove from pan and drain dry. Serve with cucumber slices.

FRIED IKAN BILIS
FRIED ANCHOVIES

- 100 gm anchovies
- 100 gm peanuts
- 2 tbsps tamarind (mixed with 120mℓ water, strain liquid for use)
- 1 tbsp sugar
- 10 tbsps oil

Grind together:
- 15 dried chillies (soaked, washed and seeded)
- 15 shallots
- 1 tsp shrimp paste (belachan)

Heat the saucepan till hot. Add 6 tablespoons oil and when sizzling hot, lower the heat. Stir fry the peanuts till slightly brown. Remove from saucepan and drain dry.

Using the same oil in the saucepan, stir fry the anchovies until crispy. Drain dry and discard the oil.

Add 4 tablespoons of oil to the saucepan and when hot, stir fry the ground ingredients till fragrant. Add the tamarind water and then the sugar. Allow it to simmer till the sauce thickens slightly. Remove from the heat to cool. Stir in the fried anchovies and peanuts. Serve.

CHICKEN KORMA
CHICKEN CURRY (LESS SPICY)

1	chicken (1½kg) cut into serving pieces
450	ml coconut milk (add 300ml water to 1 grated coconut, squeeze mixture for coconut milk)
1	tsp salt
2	tbsps cooking oil
2	cm length ginger (finely sliced)
10	shallots (finely sliced)
3	cloves garlic (chopped)
1	stick cinnamon (4cm length)
3	whole cloves

Grind together:

1	tbsp coriander powder
1	tsp white peppercorns
1	tsp fennel seeds
½	tsp tumeric powder

Heat the saucepan till hot. Add the oil and when hot, lower the heat. Stir fry the shallots, ginger and garlic till golden brown. Add the cinnamon, cloves and ground spices and stir fry gently for another 3 minutes. Add the chicken pieces and salt, ensuring that the chicken pieces are evenly coated with the mixture. Stir fry for a further 5 minutes.

Slowly add the coconut milk and simmer uncovered till the chicken pieces are tender.

AYAM PANGANG
GRILLED CHICKEN

---

   1   chicken (1½kg) cut into serving pieces
600 ml coconut milk (add 450ml water to 1 grated coconut,
       squeeze mixture for coconut milk)
   1   stalk lemon grass (bruised, discard outer green layer,
       use white portion only)
   1   piece tumeric leaf
   4   lime leaves
   1   tsp salt

Grind together:
   5   cloves garlic
10 shallots
   3   cm length ginger
   8   slices galangal
   3   cm length tumeric

Place all the ingredients in a pot, except the chicken pieces and bring to a boil over medium heat. Add the chicken pieces, stirring constantly. Lower the heat and simmer. When the chicken is tender, remove from the stove.

Remove the chicken pieces from the gravy and grill the meat in a hot oven or over a charcoal fire till it is cooked. Continue to simmer the remaining gravy till it thickens. Spread the thickened gravy over the grilled chicken and serve.

AYAM MASAK MERAH
CHICKEN IN SPICY SAUCE

1	chicken (1½kg) cut into serving pieces
250	ml coconut milk (add 100ml water to 1 grated coconut, squeeze mixture for coconut milk)
1	stalk lemon grass (bruised, discard outer green layer, use white portion only)
5	cm length galangal (crushed)
½	piece tumeric leaf
2	pieces lime leaves
½	tsp salt

Grind together:

10	shallots
5	cloves garlic
15	fresh red chillies (seeded)
3	cm length ginger
3	cm length tumeric

Place all the ingredients, except the chicken pieces, in a pot. Cook over low heat, stirring constantly. Add the chicken pieces and turn up the heat. Stir well till the mixture reduces to a smooth textured gravy. Lower the heat and cook slowly, simmering uncovered till the chicken is tender.

AYAM GORENG PADANG
FRIED CHICKEN

- 1 chicken (1½kg) cut into large serving pieces
- 2 pieces lime leaves
- 1 stalk lemon grass (bruised, discard outer green layer, use white portion only)
- 1 tsp tamarind (mixed with 2 tbsps water, strain liquid for use)
- 1 tsp palm sugar
- 10 tbsps oil

Grind together:
- 6 shallots
- 2 cloves garlic
- 3 cm length young root ginger
- 2 slices galangal

Marinade:
- 2 tsps coriander powder
- 1 tsp tumeric powder
- 1 tsp salt

Marinate the chicken pieces with the tumeric powder, coriander powder and salt. Set aside for 2 hours.

Place the ground ingredients, tamarind water and palm sugar in a pot and cook over low heat. Stir constantly, taking care it does not burn. Simmer for about 2 minutes.

Add the chicken pieces and cook uncovered for another 20 minutes till the chicken is tender and the liquid is reduced, coating the chicken pieces well. Remove the chicken pieces from the pot, shaking off the excess liquid. Deep fry the chicken pieces in hot oil till brown and crispy. Drain off the oil.

Serve the chicken with sambal sauce if desired.

SAMBAL SAUCE

- 20 fresh chilli padi (thickly sliced)
- 2 tbsps palm sugar (chopped)
- 1 tbsp tamarind (mixed with 3 tbsps water, strain liquid for use)
- 2 tsps salt
- 2 tbsps oil

Grind together:
- 100 gm fresh red chillies (seeded)
- 20 shallots
- 5 cloves garlic
- 1 tbsp shrimp paste (belachan)
- 1 tomato

Heat the saucepan till hot. Add the oil and when hot, lower the heat and stir fry the ground ingredients till fragrant. Add the chopped palm sugar, tamarind water and chilli padi. Stir fry for a further 1 or 2 minutes.

AYAM RENDANG
CHICKEN PREPARED IN A CREAMY COCONUT GRAVY

- 1 chicken (1½kg) cut into serving pieces
- 700 mℓ coconut milk (add 500mℓ water to 1½ grated coconut, squeeze mixture for coconut milk)
- 1 stalk lemon grass (bruised, discard outer green layer, use white portion only)
- 3 cm length galangal
- 2 pieces tamarind fruit
- ½ tsp salt

Grind together:
- 15 dried or fresh red chillies (soaked, washed and seeded)
- 3 cm length tumeric
- 13 shallots
- 3 cm length ginger

Add:
- ½ tsp cumin powder
- 2 tsps coriander powder

Place all the ingredients, except the chicken pieces, in a pot. Cook over low heat, stirring constantly to obtain a smooth gravy. Add the chicken pieces, mixing them well with the rest of the ingredients. Turn up the heat and bring to a boil. Lower the heat and simmer uncovered till the meat is cooked and the gravy thickens.

RENDANG PADANG
BEEF IN A DRY CURRY SAUCE

- 600 gm beef (shin or rump) cut into cubes
- 1.3 ℓ coconut milk (add 1.2ℓ water to 1 grated coconut, squeeze mixture for coconut milk)
- 2 tbsps chilli powder
- 2 stalks lemon grass (bruised, discard outer green layer, use white portion only)
- 1 piece tumeric leaf
- 4 pieces lime leaves
- 1 tsp salt

Grind together:
- 10 cloves garlic
- 15 shallots
- 7 cm length ginger
- 7 cm length galangal

Combine all the ingredients, except for the beef, in a pot. Bring to a boil, then add the meat. Lower the heat.

Continue to cook over low heat, simmering uncovered till the liquid is reduced by half.

Continue to simmer, stirring constantly to ensure the meat and gravy do not burn. Cover the pot, simmer till the gravy thickens and the meat is tender. The whole cooking process takes about 1 hour.

CURRY KAMBING
MUTTON CURRY

- 500 gm mutton (cut into cubes)
- ½ tbsp tamarind (½ tsp tamarind mixed with ½ tbsp water, strain liquid for use)
- 1 stalk lemon grass (bruised, discard outer green layer, use white portion only)
- ½ piece tumeric leaf
- 1 piece lime leaf
- 100 ml thick coconut milk (add 50ml water to 1 grated coconut, squeeze mixture for thick coconut milk)
- 850 ml thin coconut milk (add 700ml water to the same 1 grated coconut, squeeze mixture for thin coconut milk)
- 1 tsp salt
- 3 tbsps cooking oil

Grind together:
- 3 slices galangal
- 3 slices ginger
- 5 dried red chillies (soaked, washed and seeded)
- 5 shallots
- 2 slices tumeric
- 2 cloves garlic
- 1 stalk lemon grass (discard outer green layer, use white portion only)

Add:
- ¼ tsp cinnamon powder
- 1 tsp coriander powder
- ¼ tsp fennel powder
- ¼ tsp cumin powder
- ¼ tsp nutmeg powder

Marinate meat with tamarind water and salt. Leave aside for 1 hour.

Heat the saucepan till hot. Add the oil and when sizzling hot, lower the heat and stir fry the ground ingredients till fragrant. Add the meat and stir fry till it has absorbed the ground ingredients well.

Slowly add the thin coconut milk. Next, add the tumeric leaf, lime leaf and lemon grass. Bring to a boil, then lower the heat and allow it to simmer till the meat is tender. Add the thick coconut milk and continue to simmer till the gravy thickens.

DAGING PANGGANG
ROASTED BEEF

- 500 gm beef (thickly sliced into 1cm width pieces)
- 900 ml coconut milk (add 750ml water to 1 grated coconut, squeeze mixture for coconut milk)
- 1 stalk lemon grass (bruised, discard outer green layer, use white portion only)
- 1 piece tumeric leaf
- 2 pieces lime leaves
- 1 tsp salt

Grind together:
- 5 cloves garlic
- 10 shallots
- 6 cm length galangal
- 3 cm length ginger
- 3 cm length tumeric

Place all the ingredients, except for the beef, into a pot and bring to a boil. Add the meat. Lower the heat and simmer, stirring constantly, till the gravy is smooth. Continue to boil till the oil breaks out from the gravy.

Remove the meat from the pot and bake it in the oven till crisp. Continue to simmer the gravy till it reduces and thickens. Spread it over the beef and serve.

UDANG KELIO
PRAWNS IN SPICY SAUCE

500 gm medium sized prawns
375 mℓ coconut milk (add 225mℓ water to 1 grated coconut, squeeze mixture for coconut milk)
1 piece tumeric leaf
2 pieces lime leaves
1 stalk lemon grass (bruised, discard outer green layer, use white portion only)
6 cm length galangal (bruised)
1 tsp salt

Grind together:
6 shallots
3 cloves garlic
12 fresh red chillies (seeded)
3 cm length ginger
3 cm length tumeric

Trim the feelers and legs of the prawns. Wash and drain dry. Leave aside.

Place all the ingredients, except for the prawns, in a pot. Bring to a boil over medium heat. Add the prawns, stirring constantly. Cook, uncovered till the prawns are cooked and the gravy thickens.

SOTONG SAMBAL
CUTTLEFISH IN SPICY SAUCE

250	gm medium sized cuttlefish
½	tbsp tamarind (mixed with 25mℓ water, strain liquid for use)
150	mℓ coconut milk (add 100mℓ water to ¼ grated coconut, squeeze mixture for coconut milk)
1	stalk lemon grass (bruised, discard outer green layer, use white portion only)
½	tsp salt
½	tsp sugar
2	tbsps oil

Grind together:

6	shallots
2	fresh red chillies (seeded)
6	dried chillies (soaked, washed and seeded)
2	candlenuts
2	slices tumeric or ¼ tsp tumeric powder
1	tsp shrimp paste (belachan)

To prepare cuttlefish: Pull off heads, discard eyes, bone and ink sac. Wash clean and remove ink. Cut into ½cm rings.

Heat the saucepan till hot. Add the oil and when sizzling hot, lower the heat and stir fry the ground ingredients till fragrant. Add the tamarind water and stir fry for 1 minute.

Add the coconut milk, lemon grass, sugar and salt to taste. When the gravy thickens, add the cuttlefish. Lower the heat to simmer uncovered for a further 10 minutes or till cooked.

SAYUR LODAY
VEGETABLES COOKED IN SPICY COCONUT MILK

- 300 gm turnip
- 150 gm cabbage
- 150 gm long beans
- 150 gm carrots
- 2 large pieces beancurd cakes (tau kwa) cut into 8 triangular pieces
- 2 tbsps dried prawns (washed in hot water, soaked to soften then coarsely ground)
- 1.2 ℓ coconut milk (add 1ℓ water to 1 grated coconut, squeeze mixture for coconut milk)
- 1 tsp salt
- 2 tbsps cooking oil

Grind together:
- 4 candlenuts
- 18 shallots
- 14 dried chillies (soaked, washed and seeded)

Add:
- ½ tsp tumeric powder
- 6 cm length galangal (mashed)

To prepare vegetables: Skin the turnip, wash and slice into strips (½ x 6cm). Tear the cabbage leaves into small pieces. Cut the long beans to 5cm length pieces. Skin the carrots into strips (½ x 6cm).

Heat the saucepan till hot. Add the oil and when sizzling hot, lower the heat. Stir fry the beancurd cakes. Remove from the oil and set aside.

Stir fry the ground ingredients with the remaining oil for 1 minute. Add the dried prawns and stir fry till fragrant. Add a ladle of coconut milk. Stir fry for a while before adding the vegetables. Add the rest of the coconut milk. Bring to a boil and continue stirring. Add the salt. Lower the heat and simmer till the vegetables are cooked.

TERONG GORENG
AUBERGINES TOPPED WITH FRESH RED CHILLI

- ½ kg aubergines (brinjals) cut each into 2 strips lengthwise and lightly scratch the cut surface with a knife
- 1 tsp sugar
- ½ tsp salt
- 3 tbsp oil

Marinade for aubergines:
- ½ tsp tumeric powder
- ½ tsp salt

Grind together:
- 10 shallots
- 3 cloves garlic
- 10 fresh red chillies (seeded)

Heat the saucepan till hot. Add the oil and when sizzling hot, lower the heat and add the marinated aubergines. Stir fry till it softens and is cooked. Remove from the oil and set aside.

Pour most of the leftover oil away, leaving a little in the saucepan. Use this remaining oil to gently fry the ground ingredients for 1 minute. Add salt and stir fry till fragrant.

Remove from heat to cool slightly before pouring it over the cooked aubergines. Serve.

SAMBAL TELUR
EGGS IN SPICY SAUCE

- 8 eggs (hard boiled and shelled)
- 6 tbsps coconut milk (squeeze extract from ¼ grated coconut or use 6 tbsps UHT milk)
- 1 tbsp tomato sauce (ketchup)
- 1 tsp lemon juice (or ½ tsp tamarind mixed with 1 tsp water, strain liquid for use)
- 1 tsp sugar
- ½ tsp salt
- 4 tbsps oil

Grind together:
- 6 fresh red chillies (seeded)
- 6 dried red chillies (soaked, washed and seeded)
- 1 slice ginger
- 10 shallots

Heat the saucepan till hot. Add the oil and when sizzling hot, lower the heat and stir fry the ground ingredients till fragrant. Add the tomato sauce and stir fry for another minute. Add the tamarind water (or lemon juice), eggs, sugar and salt and cook for a further 4 minutes. Lower the heat.

Pour in the milk. Simmer uncovered till the gravy thickens and the oil floats on the surface.

Note: Fried beancurd (tau kwa) can be used instead of eggs. 4 pieces of beancurd cut into wedges. Pat dry before deep frying.

SAMBAL KACHANG PANJANG
LONG BEANS IN SPICY COCONUT MILK

- 300 gm long beans (cut into 4cm length pieces)
- 150 gm small prawns (shelled and cleaned)
- 250 ml coconut milk (add 200ml water to ¼ grated coconut, squeeze mixture for coconut milk)
- ½ tsp salt
- 2 tbsps oil

Grind together:
- 4 candlenuts
- 10 shallots
- 4 large fresh red chillies (seeded)
- ½ tsp shrimp paste (belachan)

Heat the saucepan till hot. Add the oil and when sizzling hot, lower the heat and stir fry the ground ingredients till fragrant.

Add the prawns.

Pour in a little coconut milk to prevent the ingredients from burning and stir fry for 1 or 2 minutes. Add the long beans, salt and the remaining coconut milk. Simmer uncovered till cooked.

KACHANG PANJANG GORENG
FRIED LONG BEANS

300 gm long beans (cut into 4cm length pieces)
2 tbsps dried prawns (washed in hot water, soaked to soften then coarsely ground)
2 fresh red chillies (sliced into thin strips)
1 big onion (sliced)
3 cloves garlic (thinly sliced)
½ tsp salt
¼ tsp sugar
2 tbsps oil

Heat the saucepan till hot. Add the oil and when sizzling hot, add the sliced onion and garlic.

Stir fry till it softens. Add the ground dried prawns and stir fry till fragrant. Next, add the salt and sugar, red chillies and finally the long beans. Stir fry till cooked.

ACHAR NANAS
PICKLED PINEAPPLE

- ½ pineapple
- 2 fresh red chillies (seeded and finely chopped)
- 2 tbsps sugar
- ½ tsp salt
- 1 stick cinnamon (6cm length)
- 2 whole cloves

Remove the skin and eyes of the pineapple. Cut away the core. Cut the fruit lengthwise into long slices, then cut it crosswise into bite-sized triangles.

Place the pineapple pieces in a saucepan. Add the chopped chillies, sugar, salt, cinnamon stick and cloves to the pineapple and cook for 20 minutes on medium heat. Stir occasionally. The pineapple pieces should be soft when cooked.

This dish can be served both hot or at room temperature, as an accompaniment to rich and creamy dishes.

ACHAR BENING
PICKLED CUCUMBER SALAD

2 cucumbers
2 fresh red chillies (seeded and thinly sliced)
1 big onion (sliced thinly in rings)
2 tbsps sugar
2 tbsps vinegar
½ tsp salt

Skin and thinly slice the cucumber. Sprinkle salt over it and allow it to stand for 15 minutes to retain its crunchy texture. Press lightly and drain off the excess liquid.

Make a dressing with the vinegar and sugar. Combine this with the cucumber slices, sliced chillies and onion rings.

Serve it chilled, as an accompaniment to rich and creamy dishes.

Shopping list:

Guest list:

Rice & Noodles

NASI LEMAK
STEAMED COCONUT RICE

- 1 kg rice (washed and soaked in water overnight)
- 580 mℓ coconut milk (add 450mℓ water to 1 grated coconut, squeeze mixture for coconut milk)
- 2 pandan leaves (washed and knotted together)
- 2 tsps salt

Drain the excess water from the soaked rice. Spread it on a steaming tray together with the pandan leaves. Steam the rice for 30 minutes. Stir the rice twice during this 30 minutes.

Pour the coconut milk into a large pot. Add the salt. Stir in the steamed rice. Mix well. Cover and set aside for 30 minutes. This is to allow the rice to fully absorb the coconut milk.

Place the rice together with the coconut milk and pandan leaves back in the steamer. Steam for a further 30 minutes, stirring occasionally (divide the 30 minutes into 3 slots: 1st – 10 minutes over high heat, 2nd – 10 minutes over medium heat and 3rd – 10 minutes over low heat).

Serve the rice hot with cucumber slices, omelette, Sambal Udang (page 49), Fried Ikan Bilis (page 86) and Otak Otak (page 59).

NASI KUNYIT
STEAMED YELLOW RICE

600	gm glutinous rice
1½	tbsps tumeric powder
1	tsp lemon juice
50	mℓ thick coconut milk (add 1 tbsp water to 1 grated coconut, squeeze mixture for thick coconut milk)
300	mℓ thin coconut milk (add 200mℓ water to the same 1 grated coconut, squeeze mixture for thin coconut milk)
4	pandan leaves (washed and knotted in pairs)
½	tsp salt

To prepare: Wash the rice and drain the excess water. Stir in the tumeric powder. Set aside for 10 minutes.

Add more water to completely submerge the rice. Leave it to soak overnight, or at least 8 hours.

Rinse the rice until the water runs clear. Add the lemon juice and stir it well. Rinse again till the scent of the lemon juice is gone. Drain off the excess water and leave aside.

To cook: Spread the rice on a steaming tray and place the pandan leaves on the rice. Steam for 20 minutes.

Add a pinch of salt to the thin coconut milk and pour it into the rice. Steam for a further 10 minutes. Add another pinch of salt to the thick coconut milk and when the rice is almost cooked, pour in the thick coconut milk. Continue to steam till the rice is cooked.

Serve the yellow rice with Gulai Ayam Kunyit (page 23), Assam Udang Goreng (page 47) or Sambal Udang (page 49).

MEE SIAM
FRIED SPICY RICE VERMICELLI

(A):
- 500 gm rice vermicelli (soaked in warm water for 5 minutes then rinsed in cold water and drained)
- 500 gm bean sprouts (rinsed and drained dry)
- 100 gm dried prawns (ground)
- 2 tbsps cooking oil

Grind together (B):
- 300 gm shallots
- 40 dried red chillies (soaked, washed and seeded)
- ½ tbsp shrimp paste (belachan)

Gravy (C):
- 4½ tbsps salted soy beans (tau cheo) slightly ground
- 1.65 ℓ coconut milk (add 1½ℓ water to ½ grated coconut, squeeze mixture for coconut milk)
- 1 onion (finely sliced)
- 4 tbsps sugar

Garnish (D):
- 600 gm medium sized prawns (boiled and shelled)
- 8 small beancurd cakes (tau kwa) cut into strips and deep fried
- 10 eggs (hard boiled, shelled and cut into thick slices)
- 10 limes (halved)
- 100 gm chives (washed and cut into 1cm length)

Heat a large saucepan till hot, then pour in the oil. When the oil is hot, add the ground ingredients (B). Stir fry for 2 minutes, then add the ground dried prawns. Stir fry till fragrant and till the oil breaks. Dish out ⅓ and set aside for the gravy.

Add the bean sprouts and mix well with the ground ingredients. Continue to stir fry till the bean sprouts are partially cooked. Next, add the pre-soaked vermicelli. Use 2 large forks (or 2 pairs of chopsticks) to loosen the vermicelli, ensuring it mixes well. Cook over very low heat for a few minutes. Set aside.

Put the ingredients (C) into a large soup pot. Stir in the ⅓ of cooked ground ingredients (B) that was previously stir fried. Bring to a boil over medium heat, lower the heat and simmer for a further 10 minutes.

To serve: Place the cooked vermicelli on a large serving dish or small individual plates. Garnish it with ingredients (D). Pour the gravy over just before serving.

MEE REBUS
YELLOW NOODLES IN SPICY GRAVY

600 gm yellow noodles (parboiled)
300 gm bean sprouts (parboiled and drained dry)

Grind together:
8 slices galangal
3 cm length tumeric
3 slices ginger
6 candlenuts
2 cloves garlic
8 dried chillies
12 shallots
2 tsps shrimp paste (belachan)

Gravy:
2 tbsps curry powder (mixed with 4 tbsps water
to form a paste)
1 tbsp salted soy beans (tau cheo) mashed
2 tbsps dried prawns (washed and ground)
80 gm peanuts (roasted and ground)
200 gm potatoes or sweet potatoes (boiled, peeled, mashed and
mixed with 1½ℓ water)
2 tbsps rice flour or plain flour
1 tsp salt
1 tbsp sugar
8 tbsps cooking oil

Garnish:
3 pieces beancurd cakes (tau kwa) diced and deep fried
10 shallots (finely sliced and deep fried)
6 eggs (hard boiled and cut into thick slices)
10 limes (halved)
2 stalks spring onions (cut into 1cm length)
2 stalks coriander leaves (shredded)
5 green chillies (cut crosswise)

Heat a saucepan till hot, then add the oil. When it is hot, add the ground ingredients and stir fry till fragrant. Add the curry paste and stir fry for 1 minute. Add the dried prawns and stir fry till fragrant. Next, add the mashed fermented soy beans and sprinkle a little water to prevent burning. Add the potato paste and stir well.

Lower the heat and simmer for 10 minutes. Mix the flour with a little water, then add it in, to thicken the sauce. Lastly, add the salt, sugar and ground peanuts. Bring to a boil, then lower the heat and simmer for another 10 minutes. Stir constantly.

To serve: Arrange the bean sprouts and noodles on a serving plate. Pour the gravy over the noodles.

Garnish with the diced beancurd, shallots, egg slices, lime, spring onions, coriander leaves and green chillies.

LAKSA
NOODLES IN SPICY COCONUT GRAVY

(A):
- 600 gm thick rice vermicelli (parboiled and drained dry)
- 200 gm bean sprouts (parboiled and drained dry)
- 50 gm dried prawns (washed and ground)
- 650 mℓ coconut milk (add 500mℓ water to 1 grated coconut, squeeze mixture for coconut milk)
- 2 tsps sugar
- ½ tsp salt

Grind together (B):
- 1 stalk lemon grass (sliced)
- 12 slices galangal
- 6 cm length tumeric
- 8 candlenuts
- 10 dried red chillies (soaked, washed and seeded)
- 10 shallots
- 2 tsps shrimp paste (belachan)

Add:
- ½ tbsp coriander powder

Chilli (C):
- 10 dried chillies (ground)
- 10 tbsps oil
- ¼ tsp sugar
- ¼ tsp salt

Garnish (D):
- 300 gm medium sized prawns (boiled in ½ℓ water and shelled. Keep liquid as stock)
- 4 cooked fish cakes (sliced)
- ½ cucumber (skinned and shredded. Discard middle seeded portion)
- 10 stalks laksa leaves (washed and shredded)

To prepare the chilli: Heat a saucepan till hot, then add the oil. Lower the heat and stir fry the ground chilli (C). Add the salt and sugar. Remove the saucepan from the heat and leave aside till the chilli settles to the bottom of the saucepan, leaving an upper layer of oil. Remove the chilli from the oil onto a small serving dish. This serves as a side dish to the laksa.

To prepare the gravy: Reheat the oil left from the chilli. Add the ground ingredients (B) together with the coriander powder and stir fry till fragrant. Sprinkle a little water to prevent burning. Lower the heat, add the ground dried prawns and stir fry for a few minutes till fragrant. Turn up the heat, add the prawn stock and coconut milk and bring to a boil. Add the sugar and salt. Lower the heat and simmer for 10 minutes, stirring all the time.

To serve: Apportion the rice vermicelli and bean sprouts into individual bowls. Garnish with fish cake slices, prawns, shredded cucumber and laksa leaves. Pour the hot gravy over and serve with the chilli.

Shopping list:

Guest list

Actual size:

12cm
11cm
10cm
9cm
8cm
7cm
6cm
5cm
4cm
3cm
2cm
1cm
0cm

Kueh

KUEH UBI KAYU KELAPA
TAPIOCA SNOW SQUARES

- 800 gm tapioca
- 250 gm palm sugar (boiled with water to make 200mℓ syrup)
- ½ grated coconut with skin removed
- ¼ tsp salt

Add the salt to the grated coconut and steam for 20 minutes. Skin the tapioca and cut crosswise into 6cm lengths and steam for about 30 minutes or till it softens. Set aside to cool.

Remove the fibres in the centre of the tapioca chunks. Mash the tapioca with a fork to obtain a coarse texture. Gradually pour in the syrup and mix thoroughly.

Put the sweetened mash tapioca into a 25cm (10-inch) baking tin. Press it in firmly. Leave aside to cool. Do not place in the refrigerator. When cool, cut it into small 2cm squares and roll in the grated coconut.

KUEH GULA MELAKA UBI KAYU
TAPIOCA IN PALM SUGAR

- 600 gm tapioca
- 150 gm palm sugar (finely chopped)
- 150 gm white sugar
- 300 mℓ thick coconut milk (add 200mℓ water to ½ grated coconut, squeeze mixture for thick coconut milk)
- 400 mℓ thin coconut milk (add 300mℓ water to the same ½ grated coconut, squeeze mixture for thin coconut milk)
- 4 pandan leaves (shredded into 1cm width strips and knotted into 2 bundles)
- ½ tsp salt

Pour the thin coconut milk into a saucepan. Add the chopped palm sugar and stir over low heat until the palm sugar is dissolved. Strain the syrup and set aside.

Skin the tapioca, cut it in half lengthwise and remove the centre fibres. Clean and cut into 6cm lengths.

Boil the tapioca in water with one bundle of the pandan leaves till the tapioca softens. Drain.

Simmer the white sugar with the thick coconut milk, palm sugar syrup and the other bundle of pandan leaves over low heat till the sugar dissolves.

Stir in the tapioca and add salt to taste. Simmer for 1 minute.

KUEH UBI KAYU REBUS
STEAMED TAPIOCA CAKE

- 600 gm grated tapioca
- 300 ml water
- 2 drops red or green food colouring
- ½ grated coconut with skin removed
- ¼ tsp salt
- 250 gm palm sugar

Add ¼ teaspoon of salt to the grated coconut and steam for 20 minutes. Set aside.

Boil the palm sugar with 100ml water to make syrup. Set aside.

Mix the grated tapioca with 200ml water. Add the food colouring. Put the mixture in a 25cm (10-inch) baking tin and steam for 30 minutes or till cooked. Remove and set aside to cool.

Cut into 2cm squares and roll each square in the grated white coconut. Serve with the palm sugar syrup.

KUEH TALAM UBI KAYU
STEAMED TAPIOCA AND COCONUT CAKE

570 mℓ coconut milk (add 400mℓ water to 1 grated coconut,
     squeeze mixture for coconut milk)

Top layer:
90 gm corn flour
1½ tsps salt

Tapioca layer:
600 gm grated tapioca
75 gm sugar
100 gm palm sugar (finely chopped)
½ tsp salt

To prepare the tapioca layer: Mix the grated tapioca, sugar, palm sugar and ½ teaspoon salt in a large mixing bowl. Add 210mℓ of coconut milk.

Lightly grease a 25cm (10-inch) baking tin with butter. Pour in the mixture and steam for 30-40 minutes or till it sets.

To prepare the top layer: Mix the remaining 360mℓ coconut milk with the corn flour and 1½ teaspoon salt.

Pour over the steamed tapioca layer and continue steaming for a further 15 minutes.

Cool before cutting into 5 x 2½cm slices. Remove from baking tin. Serve.

KUEH KERIA
TAPIOCA DOUGHNUTS

- 450 gm grated tapioca
- 150 gm grated coconut with skin removed
- 4 tbsps tapioca flour
- ½ tsp salt
  cooking oil
- 340 gm white sugar
- 75 mℓ water

In a large mixing bowl, mix together the grated tapioca, tapioca flour, grated coconut and salt. Mix well.

Roll the mixture into balls (golf ball size). Flatten each ball and poke a hole through the centre with the index finger.

Heat some oil in a deep pan over high heat. Ensure the oil is hot and slide in the doughnuts. Fry for about 8 minutes till golden brown. Remove with a perforated spoon and drain off the excess oil. Leave it on absorbent paper.

In a separate pan, boil the sugar and water till the syrup thickens. Lower the heat and add the doughnuts to the syrup. Remove the pan from the heat. Continue to turn the doughnuts in the syrup till the sugar dries to form a white sugary coating.

Cool slightly and serve it warm.

KUEH BINGKAH
BAKED TAPIOCA CAKE

- 1.2 kg tapioca (skinned and grated)
- 2 tbsps plain flour
- 150 gm sugar
- 200 gm grated coconut with skin removed
- 250 ml coconut milk (add 150ml water to ½ grated coconut, squeeze mixture for coconut milk)
- 2 eggs (beaten)
- 50 gm butter
- 4 tbsps evaporated milk
- ¼ tsp salt

Mix all the ingredients thoroughly in a mixing bowl. Leave aside a small portion of egg for glazing.

Lightly grease a 25cm (10-inch) baking tin with butter. Pour in the batter and spread it evenly.

Place in a hot oven (180°C) to bake till cooked (approximately 30 minutes). Glaze the surface with the remaining egg. Continue to bake till completely dry and slightly browned. Cool.

When completely cool, cut into slices of 1cm thickness. Remove from baking tin and serve.

LEPAT UBI KAYU
WRAPPED TAPIOCA CAKE

- 2 kg tapioca (skinned and grated)
- 600 gm palm sugar (coarsely chopped)
- 6 pandan leaves (shredded into 1cm width strips and knotted together)
- 100 mℓ water
- 360 gm sugar
- 100 mℓ coconut milk (add 20mℓ water to ½ grated coconut, squeeze mixture for coconut milk)
- ½ grated coconut with skin removed
- ½ tsp salt
- 10 pieces banana leaves
  toothpicks

Scald the banana leaves in boiling water for a few seconds. Wipe dry. Cut into 20 x 15cm pieces.

Squeeze out the excess liquid from the grated tapioca.

To prepare the syrup: Add the chopped palm sugar to 100mℓ water. Simmer with the pandan leaves till the sugar dissolves. Strain.

Mix the grated tapioca, grated coconut, palm sugar syrup, sugar, salt and the coconut milk in a large mixing bowl. Mix well.

Divide into 20 portions and wrap each one with the banana leaf, securing the sides of the leaf with toothpicks.

Steam over high heat for 30 minutes.

Set aside to cool. Serve.

LEPAT PISANG
WRAPPED BANANA CAKE

- 6 medium sized bananas (pisang raja)
- ⅓ grated coconut with skin removed
- 100 mℓ thick coconut milk (squeeze ½ grated coconut to extract coconut milk)
- 2 tbsps plain flour
- 3 tbsps sugar
- ¼ tsp salt
- 2 pandan leaves (cut into 2 x 4cm strips)
- 8 pieces banana leaves

Scald the banana leaves in boiling water for a few seconds. Wipe dry. Cut into 20 x 15cm pieces.

Peel the bananas and mash with a fork till smooth. Add the plain flour, sugar, salt, grated coconut and 2 tablespoons of the coconut cream. Stir well till it becomes a soft dough. Add the remaining coconut cream. The consistency should not be too thick or too watery.

Place 2 tablespoons of the mixture on each piece of banana leaf. Place a piece of pandan leaf on the mixture before folding the banana leaf. Wrap it in a rectangular shape.

Steam over high heat for about 15-20 minutes. Set aside to cool and refrigerate.

Serve chilled.

GORENG PISANG
BANANA FRITTERS

- 12 ripe medium sized bananas (pisang raja)
- 6 tbsps flour
- 9½ tbsps rice flour
- 160 mℓ water
- 2 tsps sugar
- 1 tsp lime paste (kapor)
  cooking oil

Mix the flour and rice flour with the water. Gradually add the sugar and lime paste, stirring well to dissolve the lime paste. Peel the bananas and dip each one into the batter, coating it well.

Heat the cooking oil in a large deep pan until the oil just begins to smoke. Lower the heat slightly and deep fry the batter-coated banana till golden brown. Do this one at a time for each banana.

Remove the banana fritters and drain off the oil. Serve immediately.

KUEH PISANG (KUEH NAGA SARI)
BANANA CAKE

- 4 medium sized bananas (pisang raja)
- 90 gm green pea flour (tepong hoen kwe)
- 160 gm sugar
- 450 ml coconut milk (add 350ml water to 1 grated coconut, squeeze mixture for coconut milk)
- ¼ tsp salt
- 8 pieces banana leaves

Scald the banana leaves with boiling water for a few seconds. Wipe dry. Cut into 15 x 20cm pieces.

Lightly steam the bananas with its skin on for 5 minutes. Peel and slice thinly (½cm thick).

Place a few pieces of the sliced banana on each banana leaf.

Mix the flour with 100ml coconut milk. Stir till smooth. Add the sugar, salt and the remaining coconut milk.

Cook over medium heat. Stir till the mixture thickens and becomes opaque.

Pour a little of the cooked mixture over the sliced banana on each banana leaf. Fold into small packets. Chill in the refrigerator for at least 2 hours before serving.

KUEH KODOK
FRIED BANANA CAKE

- 4 ripe bananas (pisang raja) skinned and mashed
- 90 gm plain flour
- 1 tbsp rice flour
- ½ tbsp sugar
- ¼ tsp salt
- 1 tsp baking powder
- water
- cooking oil

Mix the mashed bananas and sugar in a large mixing bowl. Sift in the plain flour, rice flour, baking powder and salt till it becomes a soft smooth dough. Add water if necessary to make it into a thick batter.

Heat a saucepan and add the oil. When the oil is hot, reduce the heat. Take large tablespoonfuls of the batter and drop it into the oil. Deep fry for about 3 minutes. Turn the kueh to ensure it is uniformly golden brown. Remove it with a perforated spoon and drain off the excess oil. Serve warm.

SERI KAYA
EGG & COCONUT JAM

- 475 gm sugar
- 10 eggs
- 150 ml coconut milk (add 1 tbsp warm water to 1 grated coconut, squeeze mixture for coconut milk)
- ½ tsp vanilla essence
- 2-3 pandan leaves (shredded into 1cm width strips and knotted together)
- ½ tsp salt
- 1 stick cinnamon (4cm length)

Gently beat the eggs and add 450gm of sugar. Continue beating till the sugar dissolves. Add the coconut milk, vanilla essence, salt and cinnamon stick.

Heat and stir the remaining sugar (25gm) in a saucepan till it melts and turns a medium brown. Add it immediately to the egg and coconut cream mixture while stirring to blend well. Sieve it into a tray. Place the pandan leaves into the tray.

Lower the tray into a steamer over medium heat. Stir the mixture with a wooden spoon for about 15 minutes to prevent curdling, until a custard-like consistency is obtained. Remove the pandan leaves.

Wrap a piece of cloth or greaseproof paper over the top of the tray to prevent the steam from entering the egg jam. Raise to high heat and steam for 2 hours. Add hot water to maintain the water level in the steamer throughout the steaming process.

SAGO GULA MELAKA
SAGO DESSERT WITH PALM SUGAR & COCONUT MILK

Sago pudding:
- 300 gm sago
- 1 ℓ water
- 175 mℓ coconut milk (add 100mℓ water to ½ grated coconut, squeeze mixture for coconut milk)

Syrup:
- 300 gm palm sugar
- 1 tbsp sugar
- 200 mℓ water

Soak the sago in water for 15 minutes. Rinse several times to remove the starch.

Bring the 1ℓ water to boil in a large saucepan. Add the sago. Stir till the mixture boils and the sago turns transparent.

Pour into individual dessert moulds or one large mould. Cool, then chill in the refrigerator.

Simmer the palm sugar and white sugar in 200mℓ water over low heat. Cool and strain.

To serve: Pour the coconut milk and syrup over the sago pudding.

ABOK-ABOK SAGO
STEAMED SAGO

8	pandan leaves
300	gm sago
150	gm grated coconut with skin removed
8	tbsps white sugar
¼	tsp salt
1	drop red food colouring
1	drop green food colouring
2	drops rose essence
½	tbsp water

Shred the pandan leaves. Grind it coarsely. Add ½ tablespoon water to the leaves and squeeze out the liquid to obtain pandan juice. Set aside.

Soak the sago in water for 1 hour. Rinse and drain. Mix well with the grated coconut, sugar and salt. Divide into 3 portions.

Colour the 1st portion red with the colouring and the rose essence. Leave the 2nd white. Add the pandan juice and green colouring to the 3rd portion.

Grease a 20cm (8-inch) cake tin. Spread the green portion evenly, and press it firmly with the back of a spoon. Steam for 15 minutes.

Spread the white portion over the green layer. Level and press down firmly. Steam till the sago is transparent.

Lastly, spread the red portion. Level and press firmly. Steam for a further 15 minutes or till cooked.

Cool and when it is firm, cut into 5 x 2½cm slices.

PULUT TERIGU
SWEET BARLEY RICE PORRIDGE

- 150 gm barley rice (pulut terigu)
- 150 gm palm sugar
- 150 gm white sugar
- 520 ml thick coconut milk (add 400ml water to 1 grated coconut, squeeze mixture for thick coconut milk)
- 1.3 l thin coconut milk (add 1.2l water to the same 1 grated coconut, squeeze mixture for thin coconut milk)
- ¼ tsp salt
- 4 pandan leaves (shredded into 1cm width strips and knotted together)
- water

Wash the barley rice and soak in 300ml water for 2 hours. This is to get rid of the starch. Drain the excess water.

Simmer the thin coconut milk with the palm sugar to dissolve the sugar. Strain and set aside the syrup.

Boil the barley rice with 1.2l water on medium heat for 15 minutes. Stir often as it starts to thicken. If it is too thick, add water till it has the consistency of thick soup.

Add the knotted pandan leaves and the thin coconut milk syrup till the pulut terigu is watery. Stir often so that it does not stick to the sides of the pot.

Add the white sugar and salt and simmer for 2 minutes.

Add the thick coconut milk and simmer for a few more minutes. If the pulut terigu is too thick, add more coconut milk till it reaches a consistency to your liking.

Remove the pandan leaves. Serve.

PULUT INTI
GLUTINOUS RICE WITH COCONUT PALM SUGAR

- 420 gm glutinous rice
- ¼ tsp salt
- 200 ml thick coconut milk (add 150ml water to ½ grated coconut, squeeze mixture for thick coconut milk)
- 300 ml thin coconut milk (add 250ml water to the same ½ grated coconut, squeeze mixture for thin coconut milk)
- 1 pandan leaf (shredded into 1cm width strips and knotted together)

Filling:
- 200 gm grated coconut with skin removed
- 100 gm palm sugar (coarsely chopped)
- 1 tbsp sugar
- 2-3 tbsps water
- 1 pandan leaf (shredded into 1cm width strips and knotted together)

Wash and soak the glutinous rice in 400ml water overnight. Thereafter, drain off the water. Mix the drained glutinous rice with salt and add the thin coconut milk. Lightly grease a 25cm (10-inch) cake tin with butter. Add the pandan leaf to the rice and coconut milk and steam in the cake tin over high heat for 20 minutes or till all the liquid is absorbed. Stir the rice and coconut milk mixture at least twice during this 20 minutes. Stir in the thick coconut milk. Steam for a further 5 minutes.

To prepare the topping: Place the palm sugar, sugar and water in a saucepan. Simmer over medium heat and stir continuously till the sugar and palm sugar dissolves. Remove from the heat. Sieve. Add the grated coconut and pandan leaves and cook over low heat. Stir constantly till the mixture dries. It should not be too sticky or moist. Discard the pandan leaves.

To serve: Slice the glutinous rice into 4-5cm diamond shapes, remove from cake tin. Serve the glutinous rice with the grated coconut as a topping.

PENGAT
PUDDING IN COCONUT MILK

- 250 gm yam
- 500 gm sweet potatoes
- 4 large ripe bananas (pisang raja)
- 200 mℓ thick coconut milk (add 100mℓ water to 1 grated coconut, squeeze mixture for thick coconut milk)
- 600 mℓ thin coconut milk (add 500mℓ water to the same 1 grated coconut, squeeze mixture for thin coconut milk)
- 200 mℓ water
- 4 tbsps sugar
- 250 gm palm sugar (coarsely chopped)
- ½ tbsp rice flour (mixed with 1 tsp water to form a paste)
- 1 durian (remove flesh from seeds) optional
- 2 pandan leaves (shredded into 1cm width strips and knotted together)

Skin the yam and sweet potato and cut into small 1cm diamond shapes. Steam separately for about 30 minutes or till it softens. Set aside.

Peel the bananas and cut each fruit into 2cm slices at a slant. Set aside.

Place the palm sugar, sugar and 200mℓ water in a saucepan. Simmer till the sugar dissolves. Strain and set aside this syrup.

Put the thin coconut milk over low heat, adding the salt, syrup and the pandan leaves. Add the bananas and cook till the bananas are tender. Stir in the thick coconut milk and the rice flour paste. Add the sweet potatoes and yam (plus the durian if desired). Simmer over low heat till it boils. Set aside to cool.

Serve the pengat cold with a small pitcher of additional thick coconut milk and palm sugar syrup if desired.

KUEH WAJEK
GLUTINOUS RICE PUDDING

- 600 gm glutinous rice
- 800 mℓ coconut milk (add 675mℓ water to 1 grated coconut, squeeze mixture for coconut milk)
- 300 gm palm sugar (coarsely chopped)
- 120 gm white sugar
- 1 tsp tapioca flour (mixed with 2 tbsps coconut milk to form a paste)
- 6 pandan leaves (shredded into 1cm width strips and knotted together)
- ¼ tsp salt
  banana leaves

Wash the glutinous rice and soak in 800mℓ water overnight. Thereafter drain off the excess water.

Spread the glutinous rice in a tray for steaming, add the pandan leaves and steam for 30 minutes. Set aside.

Pour the coconut milk into a saucepan and add the palm sugar and white sugar and salt. Stir continuously over low heat till the sugar dissolves. Sieve.

Add the steamed rice. Cook over low heat, stirring continuously. The mixture should thicken and turn light brown.

Add the tapioca paste and stir it in quickly.

Spread the kueh wajek on a tray lined with banana leaves. Smoothen the surface and pack it in firmly. Cool till it hardens slightly.

Cut the kueh into 5cm squares. Serve.

KUEH SARLAT
GLUTINOUS RICE CAKE TOPPED WITH KAYA

- 300 gm glutinous rice
- 10 pandan leaves (2 pandan leaves shredded and knotted together. Remaining 8 pandan leaves for pandan juice)
- 1 tbsp water
- 200 ml thick coconut milk (squeeze extract from 1½ grated coconuts)
- 200 ml thin coconut milk (add 200ml water to the same 1½ grated coconuts, squeeze mixture for thin coconut milk)
- 6 eggs
- 200 gm sugar
- 1 tsp custard powder
- 2 tbsps tapioca or corn flour
- 2 tbsps plain flour
- ½ tsp salt
  few drops of green food colouring

To prepare: Soak the glutinous rice with 400mℓ water and ½ tsp salt overnight. Drain off the excess water.

Shred 8 pandan leaves and grind coarsely. Add 1 tablespoon water to squeeze 60mℓ pandan juice from the leaves.

To cook: Break the eggs in a large mixing bowl. Add sugar. Stir in one direction till the sugar dissolves. Add the custard powder, tapioca flour and plain flour. Stir gently in one direction till well mixed. Stir in the thick coconut milk gently. Sieve and set aside. This makes the custard.

Line a 25cm (10-inch) baking tin with grease proof paper. Spread the drained glutinous rice evenly in the cake tin. Pour in the thin coconut milk and add the 2 pandan leaves shredded and knotted together. Steam for 10 minutes. Remove the pandan leaves.

Press the rice down evenly with a big spoon. Spread 2 ladles of custard mixture over the rice evenly. Wipe the underside of the steamer lid before covering to avoid condensation dripping into the custard. Steam for 10 minutes or until the custard layer is just cooked, forming a skin on top. Prick holes on the custard layer with a fork.

Add green colouring and the green pandan juice to the remaining custard mixture. Mix well and stir gently. Spread 2 ladles of the custard mixture gently over the first layer. Wipe the underside of the steamer lid again before covering and steam for 5 minutes. Repeat with the remaining custard mixture. Steam for a further 30 minutes.

Cool. Cut into 5 x 3cm slices and remove from cake tin. Serve.

KUEH DADAR
PANCAKE WITH SWEET COCONUT FILLING

Filling:
- 80 gm palm sugar (coarsely chopped)
- 1 tbsp white sugar
- 3 pandan leaves (shredded into 1cm width strips and knotted together)
- ½ grated coconut with skin removed
- 50 ml water
- 1 tsp tapioca flour
- ½ tsp salt

Sauce:
- 75 ml coconut milk (add 30ml water to 1 grated coconut, squeeze mixture for coconut milk)
- 1 tsp corn flour
- ¼ tsp salt

Batter:
- 400 ml thin coconut milk (add 250ml water to the same 1 grated coconut, squeeze mixture for thin coconut milk)
- 130 gm plain flour (sifted)
- 1 egg (lightly beaten)
- ½ tsp green food colouring
- ¼ tsp salt
  cooking oil

To prepare the filling: Place the palm sugar, white sugar and 50mℓ water in a small saucepan. Dissolve the sugar over low heat, stirring constantly. When the sugar has dissolved, sieve the syrup.

Into a saucepan, add the sieved syrup, the ½ grated skinless coconut, ½ teaspoon salt, knotted pandan leaves and tapioca flour. Mix well and cook over low heat for about 5 minutes. Stir constantly till the coconut is cooked.

To prepare the coconut sauce: Pour the coconut milk into a saucepan. Stir in the corn flour with a small amount of the coconut milk before adding it to the rest of the liquid. Add ¼ teaspoon salt. Bring the mixture to a boil over low heat, stirring constantly, till it thickens. Ensure that it does not become lumpy. Set aside to cool.

To prepare the pancakes: Place the sifted flour into a mixing bowl and slowly add the beaten egg, ¼ teaspoon salt and the thin coconut milk. Stir constantly to prevent lumps from forming. Add the green colouring and mix well.

Heat a frying pan over medium heat and lightly oil it. Lift the pan away from the heat and pour in 1 tablespoon of the batter. Form a circular shaped pancake. Use the back of the spoon to spread out the batter thinly to make the thin pancake. The diameter of the pancake should be about 10 to 15cm. Set the pan back on the heat for about 1 minute and the pancake should lift off easily when cooked. Gently lift the pancake and flip it over. Lift it out again almost immediately and set aside. Place a heaped teaspoonful of the coconut filling onto each pancake. Shape the filling to resemble a fat thumb size. Roll the pancake, tucking in the sides.

Repeat this process till all the batter is used.

All the pancake should be the same size and shape. Serve it with the coconut sauce.

KUEH LAPIS
STEAMED COLOURFUL LAYER CAKE

- 100 gm sago flour
- 50 gm rice flour
- 125 gm sugar
- 350 ml coconut milk (add 200ml water to 1 grated coconut, squeeze mixture for coconut milk)
- ¼ tsp salt
  few drops of red food colouring

Mix the sago flour, rice flour, sugar and salt in a mixing bowl. Slowly add the coconut milk. Mix well. Pour the mixture through a coarse sieve. Spoon 4-5 tablespoons of the mixture into a separate bowl and add 1-2 drops of red colouring to obtain a red colour.

Divide the remaining mixture into 2 equal portions. Add 1-2 drops of red colouring to one portion to obtain a light pink colour. Leave the other portion uncoloured.

Prepare the steamer. Lightly grease a 15cm (6-inch) baking tin. Heat the baking tin.

Pour in some pink mixture into the cake tin to form a thin layer about ¼cm thickness. Steam till this layer is cooked.

Pour in some pink mixture to form another thin layer and steamed till cooked. Alternate the coloured and uncoloured layers, steaming for 5 minutes after the addition of each new layer. Finally, top with a bright red coloured layer. Steam till cooked.

Allow to cool before cutting into 5 x 2½cm slices.

KUEH LAPIS BERAS
COCONUT MILK LAYER CAKE

- 1.2 ℓ coconut milk (add 1.1ℓ warm water to 1 grated coconut, squeeze mixture for coconut milk)
- 200 gm plain flour
- 1 tbsp tapioca flour
- 1 tbsp corn flour
- 180 gm sugar
- 2 tsps vanilla essence
- ½ tsp salt
  few drops of red food colouring

Into a large mixing bowl, pour the coconut milk, the plain flour, tapioca flour and corn flour. Add the sugar, vanilla essence and salt and mix thoroughly.

Divide the mixture into 2 equal parts. Add a few drops of red colouring to one portion and leave the other uncoloured.

Lightly grease a 15cm (6-inch) baking tin and steam the empty tin for 5 minutes. Pour in ½ of the uncoloured portion and steam for 6-8 minutes, or till the mixture sets.

Then pour in ½ of the pink portion, spreading it evenly. Steam for another 6-8 minutes, or till it is firm. Repeat this process with the uncoloured portion next and topping it with the pink portion last. You will now have 4 layers in total, the top layer being pink.

Cool to harden, before cutting the kueh into small diamond or rectangular shaped pieces (5 x 2½cm).

KUEH KOSUI
PALM SUGAR CAKE ROLLED
IN GRATED COCONUT

- 260 gm rice flour
- 200 gm tapioca flour
- 400 mℓ cold water
- 400 mℓ boiling water
- 100 gm grated coconut with skin removed
- ¼ tsp salt
- 1 tsp alkaline water
- 1 tsp lime paste (kapor) mixed with 2 tsps water

Syrup:
- 150 gm sugar
- 350 gm palm sugar (coarsely chopped)
- 400 mℓ water
- 2 pandan leaves (shredded into 1cm width strips and knotted together)

Add ¼ teaspoon salt to the grated coconut and steam for 20 minutes. Set aside.

Put the sugar, palm sugar, pandan leaves and water in a saucepan. Simmer over low heat till the sugar dissolves. Sieve.

In a large mixing bowl, add the rice flour and tapioca flour. Pour in the cold water and stir. Then add the boiling water, kapor and alkaline water. Lastly, stir in the syrup and mix well. Strain the mixture into a 15cm (6-inch) baking tin.

Steam for approximately 30 minutes, ensuring the underside of the steamer lid is wiped dry regularly.

Remove from the steamer and set aside to cool. When cooled, cut into small 5 x 2½cm pieces and roll in the grated coconut.

ICED DELIMA
MOCK POMEGRANATE OR RED RUBIES

- 200 gm water chestnuts (skinned, washed and diced ½cm squares)
- 3-5 drops red food colouring
- 100 gm corn flour or tapioca flour
- 275 ml coconut milk (add 200ml water to ½ grated coconut, squeeze mixture for coconut milk)
- 120 gm crushed ice (1 cup)
  boiling water

Syrup:
- 115 gm sugar
- 400 ml water
- 2 pandan leaves (shredded into 1cm width strips and knotted together)

To prepare the syrup: Pour the water into a saucepan and add the sugar and pandan leaves. Bring to a boil for 15 minutes, ensuring the sugar is dissolved or until syrup is formed. Cool before use.

To prepare the rubies: Mix the diced water chestnuts and red colouring in a large mixing bowl. Ensure the colouring is evenly distributed. Rub in the tapioca flour, mixing and coating the diced chestnuts with the tapioca flour. Separate the lumps, if any, with a spoon.

Pour the coated water chestnuts into a pot of boiling water. When they rise to the surface of the water, strain and rinse in cold water. Transfer to a large bowl containing the crushed ice to make it set. Drain and refrigerate till ready to serve.

To serve: Spoon the rubies into individual serving dessert bowls. Pour in the coconut milk and syrup according to taste. Top with crushed ice. Serve at once.

BUBOR PULUT HITAM
BLACK GLUTINOUS RICE PORRIDGE

- 300 gm glutinous black rice
- 1.6 ℓ water
- 3 tbsps palm sugar (coarsely chopped)
- 2-3 tbsps white sugar
- 300 mℓ coconut milk (add 150mℓ water to 1 grated coconut, squeeze mixture for coconut milk)
- ¼ tsp salt

Wash the black rice thoroughly and soak it in water for 1 hour. Drain.

Put the rice and 1.6ℓ of water into a pot. Cover, bring to a boil and simmer for 30 minutes.

Add the white sugar and palm sugar, simmer gently, stirring from time to time. The rice should become soft and swell up. If it is too dry, add extra water during the cooking. It should have a porridge-like consistency.

Mix the coconut milk with the salt.

Serve the black rice warm, in individual dessert bowls, topped with 1 or 2 spoonfuls of coconut milk.

Option: Vanilla ice-cream could be used instead of coconut milk.

BUBOR KACHANG HIJAU
GREEN MUNG PEA PORRIDGE

- 300 gm green mung peas
- 500 ml water
- 1 slice ginger
- ¼ tsp salt
- 100 ml thick coconut milk (add 50ml water to 1 grated coconut, squeeze mixture for thick coconut milk)
- 400 ml thin coconut milk (add 300ml water to the same 1 grated coconut, squeeze mixture for thin coconut milk)
- 4 tbsps palm sugar or brown sugar (finely chopped)
- 2 tbsps white sugar

Wash the mung peas thoroughly. Place the peas in a deep pot and pour in the water. Add the ginger and salt. Bring to a boil. Lower the heat and simmer uncovered for about 45 minutes, or till the water has been absorbed and the peas are swollen.

Pour in the thin coconut milk and palm sugar. Stir over low heat till the sugar dissolves. Simmer uncovered till the peas soften. If it is too thick, add more thin coconut milk, or water. Add sugar to taste.

Add ¼ teaspoon of salt to the thick coconut milk and pour it into a serving jug. The bubor should be served warm, in individual dessert bowls, topped with 1 or 2 spoonfuls of thick coconut milk.

BUBOR CHA-CHA WITH PISANG RAJA
SWEET COCONUT DESSERT WITH BANANA

10	medium sized bananas (pisang raja) cut into 1cm thick slices
250	mℓ thick coconut milk (add 100mℓ water to 2 grated coconuts, squeeze mixture for thick coconut milk)
400	mℓ thin coconut milk (add 250mℓ water to the same 2 grated coconuts, squeeze mixture for thin coconut milk)
½	tsp salt
6	tbsps sugar
1	pandan leaf (shredded into 1cm width strips and knotted together)
2	tbsps palm sugar (coarsely chopped)
280	gm yam (cut into small 1½cm cubes)
450	gm large sweet potato (cut into small 1½cm diamond shapes)

Steam the yam cubes and sweet potato shapes for about 30 minutes or until tender. Set aside.

Bring the thin coconut milk to the boil, adding salt, palm sugar, pandan leaves and sugar. Boil for 5 minutes.

Add the sliced bananas to the coconut milk and sugar mixture and stir in the thick coconut cream. Finally, add the steamed yam and sweet potato.

This dessert can be served hot or cold.

PENGAT PISANG DURIAN
BANANA DURIAN PUDDING

- 400 ml thin coconut milk (add 170ml water to 1 grated coconut, squeeze mixture for thin coconut milk)
- 160 gm palm sugar (coarsely chopped)
- 50 gm rock sugar
- 100 ml water
- 1 large durian (remove flesh from seeds)
- 7 ripe bananas (pisang raja) each cut into 3 pieces at a slant
- 1 tbsp rice flour (mixed with 2 tbsps water to form a paste)
- 2 pandan leaves (shredded into 1cm width strips and knotted together)

For serving:
- 60 ml thick coconut milk (add 25ml water to ½ grated coconut, squeeze mixture for thick coconut milk)
- ¼ tsp salt

Boil the rock sugar and palm sugar in 100ml water till the sugar dissolves. Strain. Set the syrup aside.

Boil the thin coconut milk with the pandan leaves. Add the sliced bananas and durian flesh. Stir in the syrup. Boil for 5 minutes over low heat before adding the rice flour paste. Stir constantly. This mixture should be simmering constantly.

Remove from heat and set aside to cool. Chill in the refrigerator.

Add a pinch of salt to the thick coconut milk.

To serve: Serve in individual dessert bowls when chilled. Have a small pitcher of thick coconut milk to pour over each serving.

ANG KOO KUEH
RED TURTLE CAKE

- 300 gm glutinous rice flour
- 300 gm red sweet potatoes
- 450 mℓ coconut milk (add 300mℓ water to 1 grated coconut, squeeze mixture for coconut milk)
- 1 tbsp sugar
- ¼ tsp salt
- ½ tsp alkaline water
- 2 drops red food colouring
- 2 pieces banana leaves cut into small 10cm squares
  cooking oil
  Ang Koo Kueh mould

Filling:

- 220 gm green beans (without skin)
- 220 gm sugar
- 450 mℓ water
- 2 pandan leaves (shredded into 1cm width strips and knotted together)

To prepare the filling: Soak the green beans overnight in water. Rinse the beans and drain. Add the pandan leaves and boil it in 450mℓ of water till the beans swell and soften. Pour away half the water and the pandan leaves. Blend the remainder in a liquidizer till the paste has a fine texture.

Thereafter, bring the paste to a simmer and add the sugar. The texture of this filling should be quite thick. Set aside to cool.

To prepare the Ang Koo Kueh: Skin the sweet potatoes. Boil them till soft and mash the potatoes to a paste. Pass the mashed potatoes through a coarse sieve to remove the fibres.

Pour the coconut milk into a saucepan and bring to a boil, adding the salt, sugar, alkaline water and red food colouring. Leave aside to cool.

Mix the sweet potato paste with the glutinous rice flour. Pour the coconut milk into this flour mixture. Mix well into a dough.

Take a small portion of dough in the palm of your hand. Flatten it and make a well in the centre. Add 1 tablespoon of the bean paste filling into the well. Seal it and press it into the Ang Koo Kueh mould to shape it. Knock it out of the mould and brush over with cooking oil. Place it on a small piece of banana leaf. Repeat this process till all the ingredients are used. Steam the kueh for 15-20 minutes. Cool and serve.

ONDE-ONDE
GLUTINOUS RICE BALLS

- 600 gm sweet potatoes
- 250 gm glutinous rice flour
- 100 mℓ warm water
- 2 drops green food colouring
- 4 pandan leaves
- 2 tbsps water

Filling:
- 200 gm palm sugar
- 2 tbsps white sugar

Coating:
- 1 grated coconut with skin removed
- ¼ tsp salt

Chop the palm sugar till very fine (almost crumb-like). Mix well with the white sugar. Set aside. This is to be used as the filling. Add ¼ teaspoon salt to the grated coconut and steam for 20 minutes. This is to be used for the coating. Set aside to cool.

Wash the sweet potatoes and cut them into 6cm pieces. Steam the sweet potatoes for about 30 minutes or till they soften. Peel the skin off and mash the potato with a fork. Pass the mashed potatoes through a coarse sieve to remove the fibres. Set aside.

Shred the pandan leaves and blend coarsely, mixing in 2 tablespoons of water. Squeeze out the liquid to obtain pandan juice. Pour the warm water, green colouring and pandan juice into a cup. Stir.

In a large mixing bowl, add the mashed sweet potato and glutinous rice flour. Slowly add the green liquid. Mix well, till a fairly stiff dough is obtained. Knead the dough and divide it into small equal portions. Shape into marble-sized balls.

Place each dough ball in the palm of the hand. Flatten it and make a well in the centre. Add ½ teaspoon of the filling ingredients into the well. Seal the well and lightly reshape into balls.

Bring a pot of water to boil. When the water is boiling briskly, add a few balls at a time. When the balls float to the surface of the water, remove with a perforated spoon and drain dry.

Roll in the grated coconut. Cool and serve.

Shopping list:

Guest list

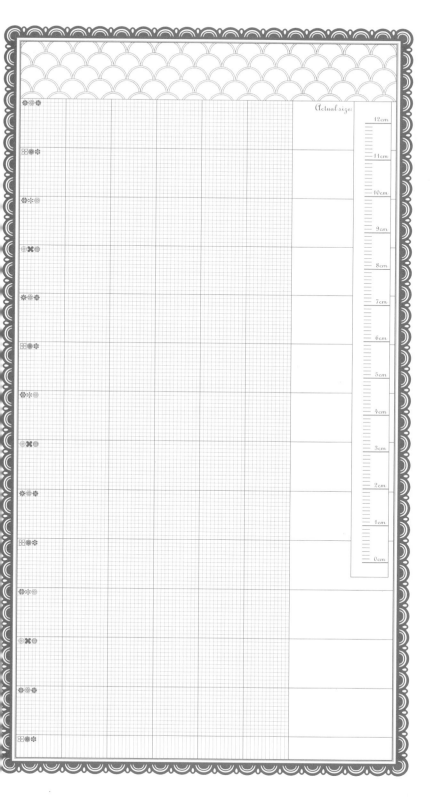

Actual size:

12cm
11cm
10cm
9cm
8cm
7cm
6cm
5cm
4cm
3cm
2cm
1cm
0cm

glossary

Alkaline Water

It can be found in Chinese grocery stores. It is corrosive, and therefore should be stored in a glass jar.

Assam

Known as tamarind. It is the dark brown pulp with seeds that you obtain from the tamarind fruit. The better quality tamarind is a darker colour, with more pulp than seeds. It is often sold in packets.

Belachan

Known as shrimp paste. It is made from shrimp or prawns. It is often sold in hard blocks, which can be cut into smaller pieces. It is strong smelling, and must be cooked with other ingredients or grilled.

Bamboo Shoots

Canned bamboo shoots are already parboiled. They only need to be scalded in boiling water before slicing.

Bawang Merah (Kechil)

Known as shallots. These are the smaller red onions. Either sliced thinly or ground with other ingredients.

Bok Gee

Known as black jelly fungus or cloud's ears. It softens and expands when soaked in water.

Buah Keluak

This is a large black nut from Indonesia. It has to be washed thoroughly, and soaked in water for several days (changing the water daily) before use. Make a hole at the smooth end of the thicker side of the nut, and use the black flesh within.

Buah Keras

Known as candlenuts. Look like macademia nuts. They are usually ground with other ingredients. It is possible to substitute them with macadamia nuts, or blanched almonds.

Bunga Cengkeh

Known as cloves. Very often used for curries and other meat dishes.

Bunga Kantan

Known as pink ginger bud or phaeomaria. Only the young buds are used. Use only the tip and petals, discard the rest.

Bunga Lawang

Known as star anise. It resembles a star, and is dark brown or black.

Chinese 5-spice Powder

It is a mixture of ground star anise, fennel, pepper, clove and cinnamon. Often used as a marinade for meats.

Coconut

It is a mainstay of many peranakan dishes, especially in kueh. It can be purchased in wet markets already grated, either with skin (brown) or without skin (white coconut). It can also be found in packets in supermarkets.

Coconut Milk

The best way to obtain coconut milk is by squeezing the juice from the grated coconut.

First milk or thick milk, is obtained by squeezing the grated coconut through a thin muslin cloth with little or no water added.

Second milk or thin milk, is obtained by squeezing the same grated coconut through the muslin, this time with more water added, squeezing a handful a little at a time.

Freshly squeezed coconut milk can be substituted with tetrapak coconut cream or vacuum sealed coconut milk found in supermarkets. But the best results are still with freshly squeezed coconut. This is especially so for use in the kueh.

Coconut milk (and grated coconut) spoils easily, and salt is usually added to enhance the taste, and to preserve it. It sours if left at room temperature for too long, so it is best to refrigerate if it is to be used later in the day.

Tip: For nice smooth gravies, cook over low heat, and stir continuously till it comes to a boil. High heat will cause the oil from the coconut milk to break, and separate.

Daun Kersum

Known as laksa leaves. It is an aromatic leaf, normally used as a garnish.

Daun Kunyit
Also known as tumeric leaf. It is a large leaf used to add fragrance to dishes.

Daun Limau Purut
Known as lime leaves. It is a fragrant leaf from the lime tree.

Dried Chinese Mushrooms
These are dark brown or black in colour. Better quality ones are larger, evenly sized and thick. They should be soaked in water to soften before use.

Galangal/Lengkuas
Known as wild ginger. It is similar to ginger, but is reddish in colour, and does not have the same sharpness. It is usually ground with other ingredients, or bruised.

Gula Melaka
Known as palm sugar. It is a brown coconut sugar, sold in cylindrical blocks. It can be cut into smaller pieces, and dissolved in hot water to make syrup. It can be substituted with brown sugar.

Hee Peow
Known as dried fish bladder. It can be found in Chinese grocery shops. It is a light golden brown in colour, is hard and looks like a dried sponge. It softens and expands when soaked in water.

Jintan Manis
Known as fennel. Looks like cumin, but slightly larger. Also usually available as seeds or in powder form.

Jintan Puteh
Known as cumin. It is usually available as seeds or ground.

Kapor
Known as lime paste.

Kayu Manis
Known as cinnamon sticks. These are light brown in colour, and are layers or bark rolled together. They can be substituted with cinnamon powder.

Ketumbar

Known as coriander. It is usually available as seeds, or ground. Fresh coriander leaves, also known as Chinese parsley, resemble mustard cress, and are used for flavouring and garnishing.

Ketupat

Known as compressed rice cakes. Commonly used in Malay food. It is made of compressed rice dumpling wrapped in coconut leaves.

Kim Chiam

Known as dried lily flowers. They are light golden brown in colour.

Kiam Chye

Known as salted mustard cabbage. Always wash and pre-soak it to get rid of excess saltiness. Over soaking can cause loss of flavour.

Kunyit

Also known as tumeric. It is a bright yellow root similar to ginger. It is available in powdered form as well.

Palm Sugar Syrup

Chop the palm sugar in smaller pieces. Add a little water and heat in a small saucepan over very low heat. Shredded pandan leaves can be added to provide fragrance to the syrup. Strain the syrup before use.

Pandan Leaf

This is a long fragrant leaf. Shred or tear the leaves before tying into knots, as it brings out the fragrance.

Serai

Known as lemon grass. Looks like a stalk of spring onion. To use, remove the green outer portion, which is fibrous, and use the inner white portion only. It is bruised before cooking, otherwise ground with other ingredients. It can be substituted with lemon rind.

Tau Cheo

Known as fermented salted soy beans. It is very fragrant, and is usually stir fried with a little water to prevent burning.

Tau Kee

Known as dried beancurd skin or beancurd sticks. The skin comes in light brown sheets. Wipe clean, then soak in water to soften before use.

Tau Kwa

Hard beancurd cakes, which have been deep fried.

Tepong Hoen Kwe

Known as green pea flour, or hun kwee flour. Can be found in small packets in supermarkets.

Tung Hoon

Known as very fine mung bean vermicelli. It is not made from rice, but the mung bean. It is almost transparent when cooked.

As a guide

½ tsp = 2.5ml
1 tsp = 5ml

½ tbp = 7.5ml
1 tbp = 15ml

½ cup = 100ml
1 cup = 200ml

1 cup sugar = 150gm
1 cup flour = 130gm
1 block palm sugar = 100gm

1 grated coconut = approximately 240g
½ grated coconut = approximately 120g
200ml coconut cream = approximately 2 coconuts

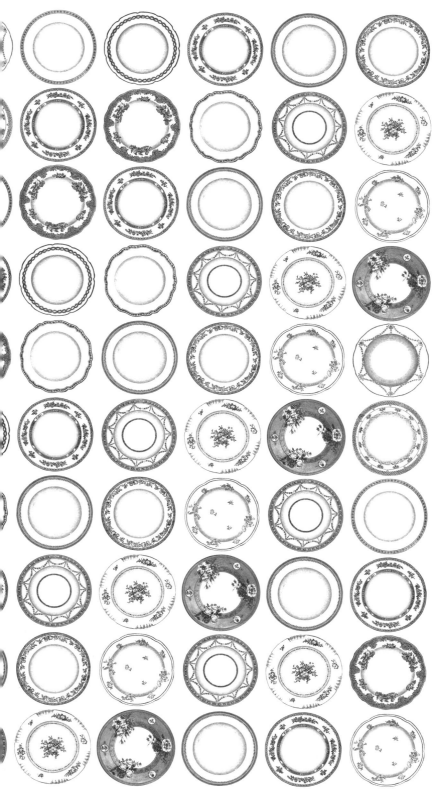